C000132733

LANDFALL 230

November 2015

Editor David Eggleton

Founding Editor Charles Brasch (1909–1973)

Cover: Emily Karaka, *Post Settlement Governance Entities*, 2015, 1000 x 1000 mm. Oil on kauri board.
Above: Nicole Page-Smith, 'Untitled', 2008.

Published with the assistance of Creative New Zealand.

OTAGO UNIVERSITY PRESS

CONTENTS

EMMA NEALE, JUDGE

Kathleen Grattan Award for Poetry 2015

The more poetry I read, the more wonderstruck I am by the genre's breadth. From digital 'telescopic' poetry on the web, to Christian Bök's biological experiment *Xenotext*, the multiple subspecies of poetry make most definitions seem as if they will break apart and spill their contents everywhere. The sturdiest definition I can dare, for now, is 'language looking at itself'.

The Kathleen Grattan Award supports production of a book of poetry rather than, say, a multimedia 'ether event'. Within this subset, printed poetry, the work I responded to most strongly still vividly remembers its musical whakapapa; it is unafraid of deep, psychological work; it attends to sensory details, knowing we live in bodies as well as minds.

The winning manuscript (among many excellent submissions) was one that had no weak or misfit poems; where nothing seemed to have been included either to bulk out the manuscript, or just because it, on its own, was a good poem, even though it didn't slot in to the brickwork of the book's otherwise solid arch.

WINNER

Michael Harlow, *Nothing for it but to Sing*
This manuscript, (its title echoing Mansfield and Beckett), also reminded me of one of Wallace Stevens' many aphorisms, 'Poetry is a search for the inexplicable.' The poems are small detonations that release deeply complex stories of psychological separations and attractions, of memory and desire. Frequently they slip into the alluring spaces just at the edges of language, dream and gesture, as they carefully lower, like measuring gauges, into the ineffable: intimations of mortality, the slippery nature of identity, longing, fear.

A slightly atypical phrasing, with a touch of the antique, often creates a sense of subtle underlining of certain *aperçus*; as do the sonic shimmers of prosody. This is a poet with such a command of music, the dart and turn of movement in language, that he can get away with words that make us squirm in apprentice workshops or bad pop songs—heart, soul—and make them seem newly shone and psychically right. The work is sequined by sound, rather than running its meaning along the rigid rails of metre and end rhyme.

The sway and surge of various meanings in the phrasing, and the way sense trails and winds over line breaks: this movement itself often evokes the alternating dark and electric energy of feelings like love, loss and the pain of absence.

HIGHLY COMMENDED

Hannah Mettner, *Fully Clothed and so Forgetful*

This collection touches on the transformations of teenage pregnancy, miscarriage, marriage, childbirth, confronting sexuality and coming out to a conservative family. This poet works delicately through cadence, lineation, stanzaic pauses, and all the internal sonics a poem can have without metre, or lock-and-key end rhymes. There is wryness and tenderness, in figurative language that sets off a reaction of surprise yet recognition; of pleasure and frisson.

Elizabeth Morton, *Caught*

Ranging from poems that have a wolf protagonist to those that deal with political trauma, this manuscript works through oblique, tangy metaphor. Stylistically, the lines are often punctuated so that meaning tumbles over the line ends, like spillage from a boiling pot, as if the poem's lid bucks up and down, but the onrush of impressions must continue. There is vital, urgent energy in this work.

David Howard, *The Ones Who Keep Quiet*

A fiercely erudite, versatile aesthetic calls on everything from mordant puns to verse drama and a syntactic parallelism that has the flavour of proverbs or biblical wisdom. Its sometimes prophetic/pulpit voice is mixed with fragmentation, unexpected polyphonic juxtapositions, disparate observations and images, as if the poems have been internally pleated. Profoundly philosophical, this work often spears existential paradoxes.

Nick Ascroft, *Nothing is as Inconsiderate as Talking*

From its brilliant, sorrowful subversion of expectations of the limerick to its irreverent, goofy, exuberant nonsense, the voice here is gorgeously idiosyncratic. A cavorting, satirical imagination hits levels of comedic joy that stand out from any crowd.

Alice Miller, *Our Machines*

From sophisticated word play to taut narrative, character portraits, and poems that show morphing, whimsical cloud-wisps of thought, this manuscript is haunted by the spirits of lost traditions. It explores, among many other things, the long wake of historical trauma, and is steeped deeply in literary passions.

Victoria Broome, *Finland*

This manuscript reminds me that what we sometimes call cliché also means a common language. Occasionally we choose certain metaphors because poetry speaks not from straining, overworked exertions to be original, but from shared, quiet wellsprings. There is, here, a deepening sense of seeing the undershimmer of an apparently roughcast, humble world—and a kind of marvel in seeing a writer's growth right there on the page.

DAVID EGGLETON, JUDGE

Landfall Essay Competition 2015

In Susan Sontag's 2003 collection of essays *Where the Stress Falls*, she aphoristically states: 'All writing is a species of remembering ... the recovery of memory is an ethical obligation: the obligation to persist in the effort to apprehend the truth.' High purpose, then, high moral purpose, characterises the best writing, and the best essay writing—not in an effort to lay down the law or trundle out strings of facts, but in order to get at the truth of a situation: to establish an understanding so that we might have fresh insight. With Sontag's admonition in the back of my mind, I read carefully through the 32 entries in the 2015 Landfall Essay Competition—all submitted anonymously and judged blind—willing to accept any subject, and eager to see what each essayist could make of their chosen subject as a way of apprehending 'truth'.

In general, the essays were very well written and encompassed a fascinating variety of topics, from journalism in the age of the internet, to the philosophy of altruism versus the politics of narcissism, to the history of the national flag, to the life of a shady Auckland underworld figure of the 1970s. One essay discussed fictionalising the life of Captain James Cook; another chronicled the early life of Robert Muldoon. There were essays on Christchurch Gothic, on retracing the Spanish Civil War experiences of writer Greville Texidor, on Jessie Mackay's Tennysonian protest poem 'The Charge at Parihaka', on the satirical cartoons of Sharon Murdoch, and on the effects on nearby communities of the new Wellington expressway.

Necessarily critical in search of excellence, I paid close attention to the rhythms of every phrase and paragraph; I was alert to narrative economy, to measured sentences, to clarity of meaning; and likewise keenly observant of awkwardness of expression, prolixity, repetitiveness, banality of phrasing, muddled ideas and similar stylistic infelicities. I favoured the light touch and wit over dull solemnity, excessive piety, a therapeutic neediness, the tone of steadily maintained earnestness that soon grates in its monotony. It may be that essayists are self-anointed, but they must find their niche. Where essayists chose to be pedagogic or didactic, then they needed to be self-aware enough to question or challenge their own approach and methodology. What was their true relationship with their subject? The truth is, the essayist is the subject, one way or another.

Winner: Tracey Slaughter for 'Ashdown Place'.
Second: Phil Braithwaite for 'War and Truth'.
Third: Louise Wallace for 'Getting the World into Poetry'.
Highly Commended: Therese Lloyd for 'There's Probably a Pill for This: An essay on addiction'.
Commended: Ludmilia Sakowski for 'Where Do We Come From? What Are We? Where Are We Going? That's None of Your Bloody Business', which is about the writer's experiences as a Polish migrant to New Zealand; and Bernie Coleman for 'What's Your Tonic?', about a summer holiday job working for a party pills supplier.

The burnished sentences and subtle imagery lifted Tracey Slaughter's essay out of ordinariness, and that poetic quality served to enhance her theme of the passage of time and its ever-shifting meanings. Crucially, her essay was no longer than it needed to be to make its argument. And, reread, it established that its ambiguity of tone was a form of moral examination, one where the conclusions were poignant rather than judgemental: Slaughter addresses some of the cultural shifts that occurred in New Zealand in the 1970s, ones whose aftermath we are still dealing with today.

The four top essays are published in this issue.

Ashdown Place

My mother is sitting in a room with my friend's father. It is the 70s. The 70s are blood orange, agent orange, clockwork, pathologically orange—but I see them in green. It would be her lime-green dress, halter neck, A-line and full length, ruched to a see-through rectangle under her breasts, a buckle of rhinestones hurting her sternum (*one must suffer to be beautiful*, she would laugh as I watched her getting ready). Or the handkerchief hem, spaghetti strapped, the skirt a green dream-catcher of Stevie Nicks scarves, sage and pear. He is sad in his ample lapels and his moustache, his disco trim of tight oily curls.

He has slipped low the wooden buttons of his dark palm shirt, and she gives a pectoral lick. Over the jungle of his left nipple there is a jade parakeet which his heartbeat moves. The bedspread is sunflower candlewick and her Maybellined lips are mild and obedient. He has started to pat the crisp split ends of her Farrah Fawcett hair with one fond lonely hand. They are expected to have sex. Unlike others in the 70s they can't yet say fuck. In fact, they just want to be married. They just want what they were bred to, raised for: the prefab house in a postwar street, its couple smiling and prospering in their decent formica future with preset appliances. They want this cul de sac to be what they thought: an enclave of satisfied middle-class pairs with matching kids. That's what they signed up for. They don't know how this trend ever got here, took over their group, this off-norm sampling, this swing. They don't know how the company car keys ever got lost in a pottery dish, how hands lucky-dipped in the tribal bowl, scraping their catch on its spiralled umber rim. *Bingo!* They don't know how to do this. But this is the 70s, late, too late.

They try to tune in, they try to warm up. From the lounge, they hear somebody lowering the needle on 'Boogie Nights', run through a programme of preliminary turn-ons. By the bed a fibreoptic lamp sits like a galactic dandelion: my mother switches it on so they watch its see-through stamens tipped by citric light. In the corner a spider plant dangles: its macramé hanger smells herbal and locust. By Boney M both their tears drip into an abbreviated kiss.

This is the 70s. All 70s memories smell to me like our one-way street, like aluminium windows and textured brick, like pineapple sun stuck hard to the suburbs, like black-flagged bugs gone crunchy and roasted in the ranchslider's bronze slits. There's the smell of beige shagpile flattened with chlorine where we play Guess Who in our bleached togs. There's our corona of orangeade grins, our milk-teeth gaps plugged with tubed-up luncheon meat we chug stuffed with Wattie's tom sauce. There are the icicle stickers in big bright webs on the doors to remind us not to plough clean through, spray our swimsuits with bursts of glass-frosted blood. And we need warning. We're hyper kids; we're all about sodastream and trolley races, swingball and sunburn, third degree.

In our cul de sac we run unchecked like a clan, stage any game we want in its dead-end safety, an asphalt ballet, four-square, bullrush, gutterball, marbles, and after we're buggered and toe-stubbed from the score we suck Tip Top or smoke candy cigarettes on concrete steps, in a six pm quiet that never lasts, *Tag, you're It!* So the 70s tastes like popsicle sticks, the sandpaper chill of that long splinter, gripping to the raspberry buds as we use them to shoehorn the last stripe of syrup off our tongues.

The 70s is lemonade, dead Elvis and the chicken dance. It's pyramid schemes and slogan tees and pingpong, Skatopia and blue eye pencil. It's suede and Jagger, it's Jemima and Manu, it's the Crewe murders, *ready to knock, turn the lock,* and carless days and hula hoops and the Six Million Dollar Man. It's the trampoline, where we try to leap the sunburn off our limbs. We rodeo and topple on its black bubblegum, giggle at the static of our tesla-coiled hair, let the dusk slow us with its wake of dads' tail-lights cruising home from their low-rise offices. It's our front garden, split level and scoria chipped, my father's roses looking wrong, their blooms out of date in the hip pink beds that should be spiked with birds of paradise or groovy cacti. It's the ponga tubs by the front door, the rubber plants under the bubbled passionfruit glass whose leaves my mother polishes with milk. And all that summer we want guns to our heads, the grownup killshot of getting our ears pierced, the butterflied dazzle of the single diamante stud bobbing in the shocked lobe's swell, a teardrop of thick infected pink. We want to be branded pretty. And one of us got earrings by age *two so four six eight* we all need them—our bodies are joined. Our fingers are spliced in cat's cradle, our legs double-jointed in elastic diamonds, our heels are jazzercised raw. We slap our sweaty hands through *under the bambushes,* hummingbird speed *true love for me*—our syncopated whacks like the walls of a mid-air house come apart at *raise a family.*

And we are the 16 children, not in a row but in a mob, the street's assorted barefoot offspring, a riot of pick-and-mix brothers and sisters, our days roadtripping through one another's rooms, the lounges and kitchens all leapfrog and swap, the benches a sudden queue for mass snacks, the pm's one nonstop tug-of-war sleepover, *eeny meeny miny* trade bunks, our feet still dimpled with the road's black jelly. We crash to sleep dopey and happy with anyone's mum or dad—right up until the end. When we don't blend. When we have to pick. When it's finders keepers losers weepers. But for now we're in the street, all tackle and cartwheel, frisbee and scraps, chinese burns, hide and seek, and go home stay home but we mostly never, hardly ever. And all the homes anyway have open doors: nothing here is air-conditioned, so you can only hopscotch from heat to more heat, the linos sticky in brown baroque with no shade to flop. The whole street warps in radiowaves of sun.

And our mums are loose too in the hot-skinned afternoon ... in the yard where the pool will soon be laid down. So every so often we ricochet around the back, up the bottleneck concrete, right by the built-in clay-brick barbecue, and there they are, stretched on the sexy complications of their fold-out loungers, gossiping and glazed. And we have to brake, and pant, and watch— the tint of their toenails, the goosebumped stubble of their vulnerable pits, their talk, their twitch. The 70s forecast is for tans; our mothers sizzle in their coconut haze, and roll their hips to bronze on the plastic-coated cane, 360, drizzled in oil. They chat and flake and bake and bask, sipping something tranquilising out of pink paper cups. Bikinis hooped with tortoiseshell, their nipples snag on polyester triangles, bright and static, so their boobs look tropical, and in the creases of their limbs they lie and roast a languid mahogany. Beyond them the bed for the new pool has been quarried in, a crew of dads, a big weekend ask. We're supposed to stay out of the line-pegged dirt; we've already trekked in too much of the deep end. We can't wait. The whole neighbourhood is counting down. But for now our mothers drowse, turn oily shades of almond and island. We stand and stare at the bullseyes of their bellybuttons.

It starts with that Para Pool. So maybe it's our fault, 21 Ashdown Place, my parents queen and king. We're the ones who dig out our back yard. All we know is, it's like installing heaven. If you sink it, they will come. We're the apex, we're the epicentre. Everything about this upmarket area, this young exec street, is capped by us. Our back yard is clouded with kids, blinking at the process: the strange parallelogram is unpacked and soon it will go down, its blue vinyl hull, its white pipes, the aluminium puzzle of its rim. My mother hosts her set, serves drinks with umbrellas, giving a smile of suburban elitism.

And then helter skelter it's done and we bomb in. The adults get no chance; it's chocker with kids. We pump it choppy, we make the water jittery and steep, a high-jump of shouts and flood. We load it with deformed buoys of plastic animals, fat bobbing rings we duck and skid through, wearing them melting like wrinkled tutus, huffing on their clear leaky nipples with chlorinated snot. The splashes whack the laundry on its rotary wire, soak the guinea pig cage so he freaks on his cabbage halfshell. All our days turn a parabolic blue—slapped in the corners of everyone's bedrooms there is always a batch of shucked togs to haul back still clammy, a dance of squeaks up our torsos. We never get out: when our mums call time we whine and skive. We burn the colour of birthmarks. Through our eyelids the world is bloodshot with sun, trippy, a veined tangerine. When we finally give in to sleep, we wake sunstruck, our nerve ends seizing with heat, and scalps tight with high-pitched sting. No matter, back in. And under—the blue an anchor in our eardrums, skulls somersaulting in slowmo thunder. Then chill, coast in it, heavy limbed, like it's all only a memory of blue, hairline shadows in the deep end below us. Sometimes if we've let it go quiet our mothers murmur and slip in with us: siesta in the aquamarine.

The men come home in their company cars. The 70s turn overcast. But not at first. At first we're buzzed that the adults want a pool party. There's all the kitsch of a 70s suburban do to help our mothers plan: there's the pyro wonder of the fondue pot with its bunsen flame and colour-coded prongs, there's the booze in the mirror-backed balsa-wood cabinet with the faux baroque cherub pissing soda from his cut-glass flask, there's the barbecue apron with the cartoon lingerie on it, the incense to stake into walnut altars, there's the Tupperware, the rainbow-coloured cocktail tumblers, the bamboo placemats to unroll, the space-age turntable to jack up with groovy LPs.

There's our mothers to watch for hours as they pencil their faces into place in their three-way mirrors, their lashes in Mary Quant sticks, their lips plush, their frosted hair kitteny. They let us crayon our own lids ultramarine, blinking at our decaled irises. They let us gloss our mouths like canned fruit, spurt our pulse-points with gusts of Charlie perfume. Then we get the job of stocking the lounge with balloons, flicking their bright umbilicals, and winding ourselves as the colour's squeezed see-through, the globe creaking wide in our cross-eyed breath, or quirking back into our lungs with a hot rubber cough. We tether them with knots of string and stage a floaty warfare.

And then the parents come. We watch them. They're models, they're gods. My parents are beautiful people, with a sitcom cast of friends. There are women in slingbacks and maxi dresses: their collarbones gleam and there are chopsticks in their hair. Someone has a burly dad whose sideburns are a big deal. The black pixie cut on one woman is trimmed with wild enamelled earrings. The dad we love most has Travolta'd his hair and his mustard flares weather around the crotch in boogie lines. He is the one who snuggles all our mums, so they giggle at his stubble, his gold tooth glinting with jokes, his chest a crackling polyester dragon. My mother swats his slick hands and gulps under her black velvet choker like the second-best woman from Abba. Her stiff dress is daisy print, the colour of corn. She's counted calories until she's a wishbone. My father's comb-over is cancelled by his salary and the aftershave she buys him.

They are the last of the 70s—they are really the 80s waiting to be, they are earners, they are thirty-something, upwardly mobile, they are pre-formed yuppies. But for now there's a little of the 70s left, that tinge that almost missed them, that taste they never got ... before they paired off, booked in their middle-class lives, applied for solid jobs and steady kids. To think the 70s almost skipped them, almost never happened here, the real buzz, the real freedom. But they've heard of it now, it's trickled down, the rumour, the craze, like dance steps. In the lounge our mothers bus stop and Brooklyn hustle, bumping their hips like fuel, and when the fever goes freestyle they flick their clip-on earrings at their husbands, who tip their pina coladas back hard.

We get bored, eventually. We're like refugees: we've been told, no way, no how, tonight we're out of that pool. The parents pull rank. So once we've trawled eye level through the dunes of food, our gums glued with potato salad, once we've rinsed our giggles with dregs of booze we swig from the gods' abandoned glasses, once a ball's been booted and the rules turn to shrugs and the teams curb drift and wander off, we feel marooned. It's mosquito hour, and the cooling asphalt just smells sad. We traipse. The street goes on forever. The power-line vibrato sounds like the test pattern globe on TV when there's nothing to see. The fizzy noise of our parents' fun is wrong in the distance, anticlockwise. We know they're climbing in the pool now because the water waves their voices. We lie on the tramp, not even bothering to scuff our sunburn on its black gully.

So we're not hard to put to sleep. There's some top and toe rustling, a half-hearted sleeping bag race. But in the end we doss down. The room's ventilated with giggles and pinches and squirms for a while, the whispers rising like stars. Then the inevitable dad stomps into the rumpus. His leathery voice lays the law, shuts us down. Or else. So the snickers don't last, the torches get clicked. We give up. And it's more than one party we sleep through. We must sleep through weeks, through long months, years even: hallways away our parents echo in their newfound cool, the stereo rattles, they gather loud and frequent, our house the new hub, with its sunken lounge, its para glamour. We get used to it.

But somewhere we wake. I don't know what wakes us. I don't know who sees when or what. But I do know I'm not alone in the memory, by the back ranchslider. The head height sticker explodes on the glass so we don't hurt ourselves on things we can't see. We just want to know our parents are out there, lilos adrift and low like their glasses, late-night voices dialled to a lull, light sidewinding on the pool from a lazy moon. Just the background of the known, the always-has-been, that's what we need. We're just checking. We just need to test, and then we'll be good, pad back to bed, duck under our zip-ups. But the radar of the voices is off, past the glass. It bends and we can't follow it. In memory the camera doesn't know what's coming—it's not moving like it knows what to frame, where to zoom. It's fixed on a curtain of beads—but that's just fear—where bodies move like mercury. We feel the lens of the water flex. Dying blow-up animals are camped on the deck, lopsided, starlit, like IVs someone cut. The pool has skinned everyone. Dads have hogged the wrong mums. They struggle, like they're stuck in someone else's clothes. And maybe the boy with me sees it first. Because the tears tip his head back hard as a blood nose. I don't know: in the memory he might be my brother.

But it's the girls I remember, more clearly, one night. We've broken off like atoms to play in the pink, the games the boys can't take, sissy. Our fingernails are lined with glitter and Playdoh is squished into the carpet with swirls of grit. Our shins prickle on their pastel radius. Our toy cash register is stuffed with tokens, silver bell cocked. The Made in China notes make us millionaires. We play shops, tag dollar signs on everything, fire sale, rockbottom. Then set up the dolls. But the dolls are going wrong. The stories our dolls star in are turning soapy and porno. We don't know why, but we bob their plastic bodies through seedy episodes, frocks sick and rigged. We noose their flaxen hair and wheel their irreversible faces, peekaboo in one another's smooth Vs, forced acts we haven't seen we have we can't we have we. Our breath feels callused. We play on, mean. Their games are in our bellies with the barbecue, make us want to puke. When they're shelved later in their goofy frills our dolls don't talk. And neither do we.

We don't know we know. All that summer we fold fortune tellers, telescope paper into pods that fit our fingers and thumbs, *pick a number, pick a colour*, so the world moves in triangles of origami fate. We quiz our mothers and fold out the felt-tipped destinies, every shuffle leading to love. And sometimes on the margins of parties we joke about who should have got married to who, because anyone can see that some of the couples don't look right. We rematch them like TV stars, red bikini to silver Casio, platform clogs to Burt Reynold's buckskin chest. *My mother said to pick this one.* We don't know what we know.

But by the end of the party season I know my mother's no longer queen. And as soon as she arrives—my stepmother-to-be—we can spot where the crown has gone. Everybody picks her. She wears her eyes mascara-etched, their green gone aqueous under the ebony fringe. Green is yellow plus blue, and that's who she is, the glory of the sun and pressure of the pool pinpointed in a green transfixing blink. She's from Sydney, once was a *model*. Her laugh is enchanting and coldblooded, lifting from a peach-lined pout. Blackberry lacquer makes each fingertip blossom, stretches the spaces between into a fan. She sits sidesaddle on the sun-lounger, her chin tilting all conversation her way. Freckles spill under the nylon breeze of her dress, where her breasts exhale in creamy status. And she smokes. Manoeuvring the party, there's a whole film of highlife that filters from her cigarette. You can't see it burn. Just the sheerest silver tremor climbing its tip. But you can't take your eyes from it. Her forefingers pose in the light as the stem disintegrates but holds its shape, until she taps it, a master, on your mother's cut glass and it crashes apart in a blur of minerals. It's the end of Ashdown: her single flick so targeted.

I think she starts the skinny-dipping. So maybe she brings the whole easy scene, an import from that wonderland over the Tasman? It's the in-thing, don't they *know*?: there are *clubs*, there's a *scene*. Does she offer my mother her husband, intending to take my father to the bank? Is that how it is? She understands the market. She's not the 70s embodied, she's the 80s. User pays. That's the story my mother would tell: my father is on the ladder, he's comfortable figures, annual bonuses, rising profile. My stepmother doesn't liberate, she cashes in. It's open trade, it's free exchange: can she help it if some women's stock just happens to be higher than others'? Or do they fall in something like love? After all, it lasts. I don't know now, or then. But I see her, poolside, steering her looked-upon limbs out of her gleaming clothes. The other women in the run-up have dieted for days, stand twitching at their buttons in a chilled hide and seek. The gloves come silkily off her heavy boobs and her hips halt before the first sip of the water. Starboard, the pool strobes her body. The men stand watching, helpless, on their suburban quay. It's ancient, inevitable: I don't know if there's anything else to see.

The pool is only part one of the end. It takes seasons for marriages to split, for houses to go up for sale. The swaps become messy, hostile, permanent. The trial, so cool and surreal and randomised, fails. There is a mourning, a moving away. Ashdown is over. I blame no one. They're from times, laced up and tight wound, when you got hitched pure, with no chance to taste, experiment—not even talk of sex. It's unthinkable now, that kind of repression—how could there not be fallout? They followed the formula, wed as virgins and woke in a fate that wasn't sufficient—what to do but smile in their well-stocked homes, their incompatible lives? I can't condemn them for wanting out.

Years later at Uni I will meet a girl whose parents too had played this game, and once again the swaps stuck, the neighbourhood disintegrated—like my parents they are ordinary people, not shocking, risqué, but regular and tax-paying, with serviceable clothes, dependable faces, settled in good streets conducting unradical lives. And I will also read books that reflect all this—those who dabble with 'the lifestyle' can often be conservative in every other way. Ashdown Place is never polluted with any other new-age kinks—they take on free sex as more guesswork than manifesto. In a couple of years they'll be pro-Springbok tour, shouting at the TV (because they'd never clash on the field) that sport has no bloody place in politics. Likewise, what goes on in the Ashdown lounge is somehow armchair, recreational. Monogamy is the only code they loosen, the only social more they question, infringe. But there's also something corporate about it, with the air of executive networking. I think of that lounge now and I see an echo of the conference circuit, a mood of enterprise, sales focused, calculated to boost return, raise status. Which is why my mother is put into a room with my friend's father, a joint venture, a vote by the social board. And they don't want. But they go anyway. And stay, allies in a manual kiss, inert, outdated, saddened by love for their mates. It's contra-sex, the comical vigil of false starts that's staged in that 70s room, contra-love, contra-freedom. My mother stresses they don't, not *really*, they *don't*—but, in the end, they give up, find others, because, well, everyone is doing it.

This conversation is triggered years later when my mother reads a line in one of my poems—'We used to dance while in the other room our parents traded partners'—and she is mortified, mouth knocked agape. *How*, she stammers, oh god, how did you *know*? Less because she thought they protected us, than because the need just never occurred to her. Because my parents are also from a time when children are background shapes in adult dramas. Kids don't factor, don't register in adult actions, their future shadows slip aside unheard. My parents didn't know it *could* filter to the child world. They didn't notice. They never suspected we knew. And I tell her, in some ways that is true. Because we don't *know*. You could not call it *knowing*.

But we are so porous. The feeling seeps in but can't be ordered or spoken or held in shape. The seeing, the sensing, happens—in angles, unclarities, ripples, depths, hollows, unlucid flashes—but we can't analyse it. We don't have the tools, we lack the means. It just lives in our bodies. And we are afloat in its images. Or we sink.

So there's nothing to do but drift to the pool, on one of the long dull mornings after. The cul de sac after a party is sealed and eerie, an adult-less street. You wander the plains of the empty house. Someone must have started washing up: white fins of fat congeal on the undrained sink. The smell is of stale Bluebird, sirloin and saccharine. On the brown patchwork platter, the cheese moon has caved. The eggs are halved in their mustard icing. You're not hungry anyway. The paper plates are scattered and swamped, festive as Twister discs, right foot red. The navy carpet is flecked with aqua in the living room, the brown of the dining room grapefruit rippled. You can feel the shift of knitted hues hook the memory of your feet. There's no one in any room, bottles in all, like cat's eyes. They've let some bottles drizzle themselves in candlewax, long intimate spurts.

You don't turn the TV on: it will make the noise of pylons. The only place to go is slide through the sticker, which is criss-crossed with spokes of mid-morning tree. The washing line is a crossword of other parents' clothes you shouldn't see, private and scanty on their pegs. In your blue suit you're all thorax. You squat and let your hand backtrack through the water's strange equations. It will tamper with your joints. You don't fall in. There are times ahead when you'll feel hauled under by what your parents do, when you won't be able to breathe. So now, you stay ankled in the loose blue shallows. You are paddling, and it will still loop on, endless, for chlorinated days.

War and Truth

In an interview to promote my play *The War Play*, the interviewer asked me what I thought the theme was. I said, 'The truth', and went on to talk about the way we mythologise our lives, and the stories we cling to because they symbolise a quality we like to believe is about ourselves and our identities. Sometimes it's a 'national' myth, like Gallipoli, sometimes it's a personal one, like the kind of man your grandfather was, or indeed, your great uncle.

The story of my Great Uncle Jack in the war is now reasonably well documented, but it has been embedded in the DNA of my family for the last hundred years. I don't remember the first time I heard it. I do remember how it polarised members of my family. Some wanted to talk about it, some preferred it stay buried. It's understandable: Jack's remaining siblings, the ones who survived the war, thought their fallen brother had been a traitor. His father, Joseph, once a stalwart of society—mayor of Dunedin and owner of 'Braithwaite's Book Arcade', then the biggest bookstore in Australasia—died about six months after Jack. Whether it was, as the speculation goes, from a broken heart, we cannot know, but certainly he took to his grave a profound misunderstanding of what happened to his son. They all did. That's why my grandfather, John Rewi Braithwaite, never wanted to talk about it. Some of that reticence bled down to the following generations, and created an overall sense of disquiet.

Why did I want to write about it? Was it just because the story was there, available? Was it some kind of attempt to cleanse my family of this 'stain'? Was it the startling injustice of the whole affair—the tragedy, Shakespearian in its scale?

It may have initially been some or all of these things. But I think it was also a desire to brush the edges of what we might call the truth.

Every writer is probably looking for the truth. If you ask a selection of writers they might say that's the main reason they write. And indeed, the truth is difficult to pin down, as Harold Pinter so eloquently wrote:

Truth in drama is forever elusive. You never quite find it but the search for it is compulsive. The search is clearly what drives the endeavour. The search is your task. More often than not you stumble upon the truth in the dark, colliding with it or just glimpsing an image or a shape which seems to correspond with the truth, often without realising that you have done so. But the real truth is that there never is any such thing as one truth to be found in dramatic art. There are many. These truths challenge each other, recoil from each other, reflect each other, ignore each other, tease each other, are blind to each other. Sometimes you feel you have the truth of a moment in your hand, then it slips through your fingers and is lost.

As a writer I understand that completely. I see exactly what he means, and will attempt shortly to expand on it. For the moment, though, I am interested in locating the facts, and trying to separate them from the dressing of mythology.

The really infuriating thing about Jack's story is that the facts of his wartime exploits are so maddeningly simple you can summarise them in just a few sentences:

Jack went to war, where he behaved badly as a soldier. He was sent to a military prison, Blargies, in the north of France. While there he witnessed an altercation between a British guard and some Australian prisoners. Jack intervened to pacify the situation, mostly because he wanted to pull together a petition to return to the front and he didn't want this event to jeopardise it. As a result, he and the Australians involved in the altercation were accused of mutiny. Whereas Australia forbade the execution overseas of its serving soldiers, the New Zealand government deferred to the British. Also, General Sir Douglas Haig was keen to see conscription introduced in Australia, and a soldier execution would hardly advance that cause. For those reasons, Jack was the only man executed, because he, with his poor military record, was easy to make an example of, and because someone had to pay.

This was not the story that was delivered to Jack's family. The documents at the trial, all of which exonerated Jack of any real wrongdoing, were suppressed, and did not resurface until the 1980s. Jack's parents would not have been told much at all, in fact, but they would have heard about the mutiny at Blargies, and would have connected the dots. Added to which, there was a garbled retelling of the event in parliament, which no doubt lingered in the public consciousness. One of the more heartbreaking moments is a letter that Jack's mother apparently received, which informed her that no medals were to be sent, a sure indicator that her son had been disgraced.

Myth

Sometime in the seventies, film-maker George Lucas discovered the writings of Joseph Campbell. Campbell was a 'mythologist' and his landmark book, *The Hero with a Thousand Faces*, became the bane of every film school student's existence. In it, Campbell tried to compress all the world's myths into one single narrative, which he called 'The Hero's Journey'. Lucas drew from this narrative to create *Star Wars*, and the fact that the film has endured all these years and bled into American (and world) popular culture is due in some part to Campbell's formulation. In this narrative he showed the power of myths, how they can give a set of events meaning beyond themselves.

Gallipoli certainly happened. It was, in fact, a disaster. But we have attached to it a series of ideas, or perhaps ideologies, that speak of our national character. We have mythologised the event. It has been taken as a marker of national identity: the 'hard men' aspect of our culture, the emergence of the 'Anzac spirit'. These are mere ideas, but they have come to symbolise something essential; something that is little more than a series of stereotypes, perhaps, but a country develops and grows up on stereotypes.

Mythology coils itself around a fact and then crystallises, forms a hard skin, so that the fact is no longer discernible from the myth. Then, if the skin is punctured and the fact is laid bare once again, as happened with Jack, it is often still the myth that is accepted. I think there's a reason why mythology has this power. I think 'the truth' that Pinter referred to is the result of a violent collision of fact and myth. It's a story containing a nugget of wisdom or instruction that speaks to us on a fundamental level. As such, it feels so universal that it seems to speak for all of human experience. Or at least the experience of a family or a country: its values, its most cherished ideas about itself.

This can, of course, be dangerous. Pinter was right to point out that 'the real truth is that there never is any such thing as one truth to be found in dramatic art'. One of the major critiques of Campbell is that inherent within his philosophy was the conservative notion that people don't change. It's easy to see how pernicious this concept can become, how it can lead to misuse through propaganda. And indeed it does, as in the case of any narrative that tries to summarise identity, whether national or personal.

When Helen Clark publicly pardoned Jack and three other New Zealand men executed during the war, there was a sense of alleviation: lifting of a taboo, freedom to talk openly about this story, even acknowledge and atone for the mistakes of the past. This is when I became properly interested. I was at university at the time. David Braithwaite, then mayor of Hamilton, was one of the cheerleaders, trying to reinstate posthumous war medals for Jack. They now sit in Toitū Otago Settlers Museum, a legacy restored.

And yet, Clark was wrong. It was a good gesture, but it sent out the wrong message. She said, 'These men were obviously drunk or shellshocked.' Whether they were or not, this implies guilt. They did something that is *shameful*, for which we can now *forgive* them in the spirit of a twenty-first-century mindset, an acknowledgement that it was a time of irrational decisions and actions. I can't speak for the other men, but this is not true of Jack. Jack was innocent, at least of the charges that led him to that bleak end in a French military prison. He doesn't need forgiveness; he needs understanding.

But there is still this discomfort. I feel it a little from some members of the Braithwaite clan. It's as if our family cannot fully bury Jack. His myth, therefore, lingers far beyond the reality. But that sense of the spectre of the past hanging over us can in fact be very useful creatively, and helped mould the play into its current state.

My family in context
The conservative estimate is that there were 18 siblings in my grandfather's generation, but it could have been as many as 22. Some definitely died at birth. The brothers who went to war were not saints, of course. It's said that some of the brothers stole a tank. It's said that one of the brothers, Horace, was shot in the head and continued to fight for three days with a gaping hole in his forehead. What is reality and what is myth is difficult to separate now that time has done its work and repackaged their exploits as bite-size stories, meant to emphasise the extremes of personality in our family.

My grandfather went to war as well. When he returned he played soccer for New Zealand, and was selected for the national rugby team too. After that he was a goldminer in a small village called Wangapeka, where my father was born.

Once, when I was a boy of about 10, I was playing rugby at school. I somehow came into possession of the ball. This was possibly the first and last time the egg-shaped object ever made its way into my hands, and it was probably by accident. I was astonished and dumbfounded, but also determined to capitalise on this success. So proud was I of my newly acquired possession that I ran with it; I ran and ran. Finally, when I realised that no one was chasing me, I stopped. I looked back. In my fervour I had run right off the field and some way into the adjoining one. I could see the teacher and other students doubling over with laughter.

My dad used to take me out and try to teach me how to play cricket. Eventually we agreed to give up the bat and ball in mutual frustration. To him it was inconceivable that I could be so uncoordinated: I must be doing it deliberately to try his patience. My father, like his father, was an extremely good sportsman: the two of them used to play cricket in the back yard. In trying to replicate that sense of bonding, my father tried it with me, but alas, I could never get the hang of the forward stroke.

What I have written above, about my father and grandfather, about myself, is factually true, and shows how far my genes have drifted from their founders. The mythology I inherited—of hard men and sports champions— apparently ends with me. I can no more kick a ball than wield a rifle at another man. Perhaps that's because I only own a quarter of the genetic material of my grandfather. But, in a family, your heritage is part of the myth of the self. Am I an anomaly, or is there some wrenching of the romantic and the real still to be done? I wouldn't be suited for war, and Jack wasn't either.

He called himself a 'bohemian journalist', and whatever he meant by that, I felt some affinity with him as a writer. He was not meant for war. It's not clear why he even went, but when he was there he misbehaved. He managed to become a lance corporal before being stripped of his rank for going AWOL, falsifying a leave pass and various other petty offences. At the British military prison, Blargies, the final tragic act of his short life played out.

The play

I'd been thinking about writing a play of this story for many years. I'd had a couple of tries: once as a film script, once as a TV play when I was in England. Neither worked, nor ever saw the light of day.

Why didn't they work? There are some conclusions I could draw. First, I am not very interested in military history, or the mechanics of warfare. The aesthetics, yes: an attraction to the bleakness in depictions of the trenches; that grainy film footage of soldiers in the battlefields holds a visceral emotional appeal. But I don't know or care about the ins and outs of military campaigns. Perhaps you've been at a party, trapped in a corner by an amateur military historian who will explain to you tactics, the particulars of attacks, formations, generals and battles in great detail, probably offering an analysis of why this or that campaign succeeded or failed. Perhaps you are one of those historians. If so, I recommend that you don't engage me in the conversation.

So a play set predominantly in the war was a difficult prospect for me. But also the story itself is difficult. How do you come to any conclusion about a man whose life is cut tragically, meaninglessly short by government machinations? It's an interesting story, it's a dramatic story, but it's a downer. Not that I mind that: *Othello* is a downer; *King Lear* is a downer. But they deliver their bleak message with poignancy and power. It's not that a story even has to end on a note of hope, but it has to have some kind of conclusion beyond the expected, from which you can draw no understanding, solace, or meaning. There needs to be something about it that is poetic.

Kubrick's *Paths of Glory* is a brilliant, if flawed film. Set in a World War I camp, it tells a similar story to Jack's, and it ends not with hope, but with a sort of ironic, ambiguous moment. After some of the men are executed, the remaining men gather in a barn, where an announcer brings out a German girl and explains that they are in for 'a little diversion'. The general, played by Kirk Douglas, stands outside, observing the men as they observe the German girl sing a haunting, elegiac song that seems to distort reality, twisting it into another shape: some kind of saccharine other world. The men are unaware that they have to return to the front, and the general allows them this moment of escape. It's a counterpoint, a juxtaposition, sentimentality in brutal contrast with reality, a place to transcend. This is what the men's faces seem to communicate, as Kubrick's camera probes them, measuring every tear that drops from their eyes as they are all, momentarily, stunned into silence.

A similar kind of poetic denouement never presented itself to me in the case of Jack's story. Unable ever to find the right shape for the play—and sometimes you have to talk in those terms—I put the idea aside for some time. Years, in fact. But then in 2014 a fund became available: the WW100 fund, for commemorative works of art about the war. I thought of the story of Jack, and dug it out of my memory. I talked it over with Lara Macgregor, artistic director of the Fortune Theatre in Dunedin, who had never commissioned a work before. I was given the commission (part of me had feared just that!) and now had to write the play.

As I've said, the basic story of Jack's rise and fall is very simple, and yet when I started to write the play I realised one massive ingredient was missing: the question of *why*. Why did Jack behave in this apparently arbitrary way? Why did he go to war in the first place, given that he really just wanted to be, in his own words, a 'bohemian journalist' and 'was not cut out for soldiering'? Why did he behave badly in the trenches, then suddenly try to pull his socks up once at Blargies?

We don't know the answers, but we can make educated guesses. Jack's older brother, Horace, had been badly wounded in Gallipoli. He returned home, but died soon after. For that reason, and given the military fervour in all the Allied countries at the time, the pressure on Jack to enlist would have been overwhelming. No doubt he did want to stay home, but that was not an option. He might also have been influenced by his other brothers still over there. Once enlisted he tried to behave in an appropriate manner—as mentioned, he rose to the rank of lance corporal—but was soon demoted. I have to assume, after his initial effort, he realised the whole business was untenable, and let himself slip. While at Blargies one can only surmise that he felt ashamed of his conduct and tried to play it straight. Perhaps he didn't want news of his shame reaching his family.

In any case the story, which appears so simple, is in fact unruly. Jack's arc, if there is one, wavers around like a drunk trying to walk the line. It's huge and complicated, and drama doesn't do complication very well.

I wrote the first draft in what I thought was an expressionist manner: I dipped and dived back and forth between Dunedin and France in the war. I wanted to keep in sight why the story was being told: because of those final scenes, where Jack is dragged to the pole and executed for something he didn't do.

I sent it to Lara. She read it and sent it to an outside script adviser, who came back with notes. In summary, they said, 'This comes across as just another war play. Where is the personal connection?' Lara in particular said she loved the initial story, and the script ought to 'break her heart', and yet it didn't.

I felt in my bones that something radical had to happen. I still wanted to keep hold of that energy, that naiveté that is required when writing a play, or probably any piece of fiction, especially in the early drafts. You must feel free to play: to throw things at the wall and see what sticks. You cannot allow yourself to fall into safe territory.

I try to summon the feeling I had when I was first writing, back in my early twenties when I didn't know any better (and when I was writing plays that people were excited about, probably because I didn't know any better). It was a feeling of wanting to go there, to push my own boundaries to see what lay beyond. I used to give myself a little rule: if I am going down Path A, and an idea occurs to me that would change everything and send me irrevocably down the one-way street of Path B, I should take it. Why? Because it's usually the more radical idea—it's usually the idea that takes you off the 'beaten track', away from cliché, from comfort, from logic, and plunges you into the choppy waters of the new. Sometimes you later find that this newness is not all that new, and what you thought was original is in fact not, or sometimes just a different kind of cliché, but it's always worth the experiment of departing from that initial path. Of course it also means it's working. If you're telling a story and a radical idea occurs to you, then you're invested in that story, your brain is firing, your heart is pumping. You're going along with the suffering of your characters. You're feeling it.

Something occurred to me: a play I'd seen in London some years earlier. It was called I Am My Own Wife, by Douglas Wright. It had been a huge success. One of the things I remembered about it was the playwright claiming he'd suffered a debilitating bout of writer's block that had delayed the final product by some years. The way he solved this problem was by putting himself into the text, so that the play became a kind of interrogation of the main character by the writer, on the subject of how frustrating and elusive that main character is. I took out the script from the library, to refresh myself on the play, but also in the hope that there would be an introduction. There was, and in it Wright described how someone else suggested the idea of putting himself into the text (he was initially opposed). He also described workshops, wherein he would arrive with only fragments of text, and the director and actors would bring their own ideas to the table.

I was energised and excited by this, and realised I had to do the same: I had to put myself into the play. I assumed it would be an occasional voice interrupting the action, questioning it, as in Wright's play. But that's the pleasure of taking a new path: you never know where it will lead you.

In many ways, like Wright, I was against the idea, but I think that in itself is a reason to at least investigate it. Early on in my writing life I made a note of certain things not to do in a script. One was to overuse technology. I think the theatre is a primal space—as primal as banging on a drum—and the inclusion of technology always seems phoney to me. Film is the realm of technology. The movie industry is always redefining itself in terms of technology—which is not to denigrate cinema: I love movies as much as anyone else.

But the stage is something else. The stage is primitive. The stage is elemental. It can offer a deeper insight into emotions, motivations, what it is to be human. It pares down the human experience, stripping away technology, reality, sometimes even staging itself, and peering straight into the soul of a man and a woman, emotionally naked on stage.

I don't like to write about writers. I feel this is a cop-out—a sort of hole where an idea should be, which can too easily become self-indulgent and vacuous. Many have done it and produced great work, but I always felt it wasn't for me. Related to this, I wanted to avoid postmodernist meta-theatre devices like, say, including myself in a play (anytime someone uses the prefix 'meta' I shrivel inside, even though the title itself—*The War Play*—is intentionally self-reflexive: the Phil character is in the process of writing this 'war play'). These techniques—sometimes just gimmicks—were explored and exhausted in decades past. Pirandello was the master of this kind of game-playing. Dennis Potter, the great television playwright (back when such an occupation existed), messed with what constitutes the artifice of fiction, and we don't need to go back to the Absurdists to see that these ideas are not new.

But it's important to break your own rules. Lars von Trier founded Dogme 95 cinema with very specific rules about making movies, made one movie this way, then abandoned the rules he'd created. Art is the medium of rule-breaking, and the old saying is true: you have to know the rules before you can break them. Then it's almost your duty to do so, especially if the rules are self-imposed.

When I decided to include 'Phil' as a character, certain ideas cemented themselves, and I think this is the key. I did not include the character as a gimmick. I remember Dennis Potter again, becoming indignant when an interviewer suggested that he was consciously trying to break a mould with his work—his landmark television play *Blue Remembered Hills* involved a cast entirely made up of adults playing children; his landmark series *The Singing Detective* and *Pennies from Heaven* included, as a central conceit, characters lip-synching songs. Potter said this was the one area in which he would 'stamp his feet', because he hated the suggestion that there was any intent on his part to shock or subvert merely for the sake of it. He did these things simply out of necessity. Using adults to play children was, he felt, the only way he could avoid the twee sentimentality of watching children: to push past that and see that for children, the threat of a bully is every bit as real and frightening as a thug on a dark street corner is to an adult. To have actors lip-sync to songs was a way of delivering to the forefront the 'cheap emotion' of that music, which says the world can be other than it is.

So it was for me. Although excited at the prospect, I was also somewhat against the inclusion of 'myself' as a character, and yet I knew it had to be there, because this is not 'just a war play', and what was missing from the first draft was what happened *after* Jack died. The ensuing hundred years. The effect on the family. The shame, the suppression of the facts. This was, crucially, a chance to analyse the truth, to chisel away at those hardened cells of myth and look inside. Jack had maintained a pervasive presence in our family, yet here he was now, stripped naked, looked at from the outside, his emaciated body and soul under a microscope—Phil's microscope. That is just as crucial as the story of Jack itself. It created a new dynamic: the idea that Jack is *back there*, a hundred years ago, and yet he is also *right here*, right in front of our faces, especially if you happen to share some of the same genes. The past is like that. It's both an event in time, and a reality staring you in the face.

There's a danger with World War I plays that they are about either the glorification or the futility of war, usually the latter (and the former only in a sort of aesthetic or sentimental 'brothers in arms' sense). Establishing a contemporary timeframe can help jettison those tired themes. I didn't want to make a proclamation on war, precisely because so many writers have done that already, and all have come to the same (obvious) conclusion. I wanted the war setting to be almost incidental. Drama creates immediacy—even if the action did happen back then, it's happening before you on stage. And the inclusion of Phil allows a contemporary framework. Phil becomes our tour guide, showing us Jack, allowing us to see him from the inside and the outside.

It also reduces Jack to his true proportions. He was 31 when he went to war, which is an advanced age for a soldier but still quite young. He of course became, for our family, more than just a scared young man; he became a spectre of dread. Now I had the chance to return to that pathetic and lonely figure and interrogate him.

As soon as I started writing 'Phil' and his father, things seemed to work. A workshop was scheduled, and after that I planned to go to the Edinburgh Festival. I was very keen to get this Phil idea onto its feet, as we playwrights say, but I had very little time. I mentioned my plan to Lara and she was quite impressed. I cobbled together as much as I could of the new idea, and in the workshop we went through both scripts.

The response to the 'Phil' inclusion was mixed: people felt that aspects from both versions worked, but all were excited by the new script's possibilities. There was an American woman present in the workshop, just observing. She was in town visiting friends. Afterwards she said to me, 'Some of that seemed like another play I saw workshopped, called *I Am My Own Wife*.'

As the new draft progressed, I found myself distorting the facts and creating wildly inaccurate portraits of my family. I couldn't understand why I was becoming so free and easy, twisting characters and their histories in any way I saw fit, remaining faithful to only one set of facts: those that explained what happened to Jack in that prison. I think perhaps I wanted to create an 'alternative universe' version of my family. Allowing 'myself' and 'my father' to walk the boards was making me so vulnerable that I had to fictionalise them.

The play was produced at the Fortune in March 2015. There was a lot of publicity, and the production seemed to be successful. The director commented in the programme, 'The War Play is full of lies and half-truths.' This is correct, but to bring it back to the initial question of 'the truth', I think the lies are justified. The lies are more heavily weighted on the contemporary side than the historical: the only thing I really share with my namesake is the name, and even that is never mentioned in the play. The father is really nothing like my own father. But the director's note continues:

'Philip has bravely played fast and loose with other details of his family's century-old story—all in service of arriving at some greater truths about men and war, fathers and sons, and the way events of World War I still ripple through time to haunt and challenge us.'

Brave or not, these 'greater truths' are the ones we're all looking for.

I didn't write the play to exonerate Jack, or to promote deeper understanding in my family. I wrote the play because it's a good story, and because I wanted to deconstruct the myth: the myth of the family, the myth of the self. Can these be wrenched apart, at this late stage? It has been a hundred years since my Great Uncle Jack was executed on a pole in a French prison for a crime he didn't commit, but I feel like it's right beside me, that story, that man, running alongside me. I shout out to Jack across the ages and he seems close: close enough to shout back.

LOUISE WALLACE

Getting the World into Poetry

My boyfriend is a butcher and he has to go to work real early to put on his costume.

The buses I usually ride are in commuter timeslots—full of people in sharp business attire, reading the news on tablets. On a Saturday evening in Wellington, I was on a bus bound for the city. Its passengers were captivating: youthful, energetic and dressed with great care. The scent of anticipation was in the air in the form of overpowering perfumes and colognes. Their heads swivelled in all directions. They laughed and pointed at will. It might have been infectious if I hadn't been so stunned.

Two young women were speaking behind me. 'My boyfriend is a butcher and he has to go to work real early to put on his costume,' one told the other. As soon as I heard the word 'costume' I began to overhear on purpose; in other words, eavesdrop. I concentrated on their voices, picking them out from the others on board. I leaned my ear in their direction. I typed the words of their conversation into my phone as they spoke.

I don't know how I got here
I mentioned the experience to my sister. The speed and confidence of her response surprised me. 'Google *overheard at*,' she said, as though the connection was so obvious I should have made it myself. The search returned an astonishing number of websites celebrating the overheard: *Overheard in the Office*, *Overheard at Yoga* and the very specific *Overheard at a Horse Show*. I was familiar with the concept but I hadn't expected its prevalence.

On these websites, users submit dialogue they have heard in public spaces, for mass consumption. The quotes are removed from their original context, so it amplifies their strangeness, their tragedy or humour. 'I don't know how I got here,'[1] reports the site *Overheard at Harvard*, from a man so inebriated he literally cannot recall the hours preceding. In isolation the quote gains a fragile quality; it taps into fears of life passing us by.

These websites aim to entertain. The quotes are presented ironically and ask the reader to have a giggle at the original speaker's expense. *Overheard at Whole Foods* includes lines like 'I need some artisan meats to go with my artisan breads,' and 'I'm a raw vegan but I'm still eating fish and chicken.'[2] New Zealand has dabbled in the trend with Facebook pages such as *Overheard in Herne Bay* and *Overheard at Otago*. 'I don't know how I got here' became more potent: how had this phenomenon begun?

Overheard in New York is believed to be the website that launched a thousand others like it. A founding editor has criticised copycat sites. However, looking through New Zealand's newspaper archives, it's clear that publishing direct speech for entertainment is neither a new trend, nor one that occurs only in 'other places'. In an 1885 edition of Canterbury newspaper the *Star*, under the heading 'Contemporary Humour', I find:

> *Overheard at a Bazaar*
> Disgusted Male Victim: 'Five shillings for a cigar that isn't worth twopence! Why, it's a downright swindle.'
> Aristocratic Amateur Saleswoman: 'No sir; not a swindle, only a sell.' (She got the five shillings).[3]

Whether this is a genuine account of a real-life conversation or something created by a writer's imagination, the format is eerily similar to its online successors more than a century later. It suggests a long-running attraction to collected dialogue.

It just struck me

American artist Judith Henry has worked with the overheard for more than three decades. Since 2000 she has published numerous books of her recordings, including *Overheard at the Museum* and *Overheard While Shopping*, where, according to her website, 'text and photos are paired in surprising juxtapositions that suggest narrative while resisting closure'.[4] That may be a generous description of this work's effect, but I am more interested in her impulse. In a 2007 article for *New York Daily News*, Henry explains how the initial idea came to her: 'One day, she said, I heard someone on the elevator say, "Her personality makes her prettier." It just struck me, and I wrote it down on a piece of scrap paper.'[5]

'It just struck me' is a rather lacklustre description of inspiration; it doesn't line up with how I felt on the bus. I prefer Mary Shelley's version. In the 1831 introduction to her novel *Frankenstein*, Shelley recounts that while in Switzerland for a summer she and her husband, Percy, found themselves neighbours with Lord Byron. It was a wet summer and they spent a lot of time cooped up indoors together. 'Many and long were the conversations between Lord Byron and [Percy] Shelley to which I was a devout but nearly silent listener,'[6] she says. The men's conversation turned to the experiments of Darwin and Galvini and the idea of bringing the dead back to life. Shelley describes how that night she went to bed but couldn't sleep, due to the ideas whirring in her head, leading to the conception of *Frankenstein*. She says, 'The idea so possessed my mind that a thrill of fear ran through me ...'[7] and it's that 'thrill' that captures the effect. It's a jumpy sort of feeling—a spark, a noticeable charge.

The article on Henry's practice goes into detail about her process, and it's clear that Henry's being struck is no accident. Like most writers, Henry does not adhere to the common portrait of the artist: alone in her studio, hands poised over a typewriter's keys, waiting to be struck by inspiration. This portrait implies that inspiration comes by chance, in the same way one might have the bad luck to be struck by lightning. 'Inspiration' even offers the possibility of divine intervention. Writers are a lot more shrewd and calculating than this picture suggests, inspiration more laborious. Henry, with notebook in hand, roaming city streets, lurking and listening in bookstores and galleries is, in effect, clinging to a metal rod in an open space—doing everything she can to increase the likelihood that inspiration might bless her with its touch. The key is that you have to be receptive to that happening. Have your eyes and ears open. Be *ready* to be struck.

What is this 'it'?

The problem with finding inspiration in real-world dialogue is that conversations go on around us continually. Information overload has become an accepted way of life. To be heard, a strand of conversation must not only overpower all the other sounds around it, but also pull our focus from our mobile device, shopping list or child—whatever else we are concentrating on in our multi-tasking lives. It must generate something greater than just annoyance at the volume or level of over-sharing. While the article on Henry discusses her process, what it does not explore is *why* something strikes her. 'It just struck me,' she says. But what is this 'it'?

The same week I found the piece on Henry, I read about *The Listening Project*, a BBC Radio venture. Listeners propose a conversation on any topic they wish and, if selected, are invited into the studio to record the conversation for broadcast. The producers base their selections on what they believe count as 'those rare exchanges that really matter'.[8] It follows that the producers then become the arbiters of what matters, at least in terms of this project. I was interested in what their parameters might be for that standard, so I listened. Conversations about immigration, the strength of a grandmother, homelessness and a local cemetery have all made the cut. Was the producers' vision borne out in what they were hearing? Or did the conversation sometimes seem unusual, like what I had heard on the bus? Were they amused or simply intrigued? And once they found 'what mattered', what then?

Shelley used dialogue as the inspiration for art, but the original conversation does not remain. On the 'overheard' websites, the quote is cut away with surgical precision from its source, and re-presented in whole form as an object—something to be looked at, something on show. As with *The Listening Project*, the dialogue is preserved, rather than vanishing in the air as most conversations do. What can we do then with the dialogue we collect to take it a step further? To not simply pickle it and lengthen its life, but to recontextualise it and turn it into something new? Judith Henry presents overheard lines by pairing them with photographs. I imagine this is only the tip of the iceberg when thinking of the possibilities for a poetic use of found speech.

Can this really be art?

A little to the left
Neil, that's nice, and
John, if you could come in
a bit, good, good,
now Neil, if you can turn
your body, this way,
yep, just a little, yep ...[9]

This is the opening of 'Photograph,' by Jenny Bornholdt. The poem is made up entirely of the real-life directions of a photographer, which become a sort of warped monologue. You can imagine the triggers going off in Bornholdt's brain as she listened to the instructions. It's a familiar experience—the poem is accessible. By isolating the lines, Bornholdt encourages us to see the humour in the situation, but also to move beyond it and consider the oddness of modern life. In this way the poem is not so different from the 'overheard' websites, except for the major distinction—the dialogue is being presented as art.

What effect can this have? Great furore surrounded the exhibition of Tracey Emin's visual art piece *My Bed* at London's Tate Britain in 1998. The piece was exactly what the title suggests: the artist's slept-in bed—a mess of tangled and stained sheets—complete with used tissues, dirty underwear and liquor bottles at its side. Emin stated that she had not left the bed for a number of days following the breakdown of a relationship, and she had shown it as it was. 'Can this really be art?' was the central concern. Some people were outraged; others were disgusted that such ordinary objects could be elevated to the status of art.

Bill Manhire rails against such misgivings: 'Getting the world into poetry'—I suspect that's my one big obsession,'[10] he says in an interview with Andrew Johnston. In his essay 'Dirty Silence: Impure sounds in New Zealand poetry' Manhire advocates the use of dialogue, languages and other voices, as well as making use of multiple and modern meanings. He encourages us to see that work that incorporates material from 'the world' is all the more interesting for it. While the dialogue these poems use may be made of simple language, it adds texture, making the poems complex, rich and layered. The approach works against the traditional notion of poetry as a 'pure voice' or 'high art'. I associate it with a term like 'poetry for the people', which carries with it a sense of empowerment, or further still, revolution.

There is an art to this. The way Bornholdt has arranged the lines in her poem, and possibly embellished or adjusted the original dialogue, allows for a more fine-tuned lyricism. There is a new lightness to these practical instructions and the poem asserts that there is art in the everyday. Emin's detractors had it the wrong way around when they asked, 'Can this really be art?' By using collected speech in their work, poets are not elevating the ordinary to art, but bringing art back down to earth.

The sound itself

I returned to *The Listening Project*. What if it was something other than content that caused a moment of engagement—not what they said, but how they said it? I listened again. One woman's voice sounded like bubbles being released underwater: her words competing to rise to the top, pushing in and over one another. Another man's words were sharp, his vowel sounds short like bullets.

In 'Aunty Flu', Glenn Colquhoun has been struck by a unique voice and he uses it to reveal character. The entire poem is made of Aunty Flu's speech, which implies it is the best way to do justice to her person. 'Here is a character I could not have made up, even if I had wanted to,' the poet is saying. Through her own words we come to know this stubborn and cheeky woman. She has an endearing dry wit:

> I have been to the doctor. He is a Pakeha doctor.
> He said that I smoke too much.
>
> I said 'Well doctor it is like this,
> if I walk out of here I'm still going to smoke—you're not
> paying for my smokes.' He said 'Are you taking your pills?'
> I said I hadn't taken them for a week and I'm not dead yet.
>
> He said 'O—Mrs Rewiti.'[11]

Aunty Flu's voice is also a distinctively Māori voice, and it is that feature—that point of difference—that caught Colquhoun's ear.

Recognition or familiarity can also engage the ear. Growing up with something, you may not notice its unique qualities until after a period of separation. When I go back to the North Island's East Coast, it's the candid, informal speech I identify with—it signifies to me that I am home. 'Giz a bite,' I hear as I pass two students after school, one tucking into a pie. I know this language and there is something comforting in the sound.

When a writer presents their own language on the page, the found material is not necessarily dialogue, but dialect. It's a particular way of speaking: the sound itself. If it is new to the reader, they will grapple with the dialect and may enjoy an attempt to translate the language into their own. Humour can ensue.

I speak English, and so do the speakers in William Letford's collection *Bevel*, but reading this book was a challenge. Many of the poems are written phonetically in Scots dialect:

> The labourer stood up, it's aboot strength, son
> Wit kin yi caerry, wit kin yi leave behind[12]

I am able to interpret the words, but doing so makes me work that bit harder—it's an extra step in accessing the intent of the poem and an additional level of engagement. I wrap my tongue around the words. I roll them in my mouth like marbles. It works in the same way as a tongue twister: the challenge makes it enjoyable, and failure is funny.

Come an live wif us

But that is not the extent of it—dialect's presence can do more. In a poem from his collection *The Cartographer Tries to Map a Way to Zion*, Jamaican poet Kei Miller tells the story of a visitor asking for directions who receives a roundabout set of instructions from a local:

> Awrite, you know the big white house at the bottom of Clover Hill with all the windows dem board up, and with a high shingle roof that look almost like a church?

Where you might expect something like 'turn left onto Smith Street,' these directions become more and more detailed, seemingly absurd:

> And in front the house you always see a ole woman, only three teeth in her mouth, and she out there selling pepper shrimp in a school chair with a umbrella tie to it.

Like Bornholdt's 'Photograph', Miller invites the reader in using humour and a familiar experience, and he presents the everyday as art. Miller's 'everyday' is a Jamaican dialect that fuses with and negates traditional English. After more of the local's directions, the poem ends with a twist:

> Yes, yes, the cartographer insists. I know it.
> Good, says the I-formant. Cause you mustn' go there.[13]

The conclusion is good-natured and it is funny because it's unexpected; Miller invites the reader in, only to challenge them. The literal reading is that the cartographer should not go to this place for their own safety, but it is undercut by a larger idea: that there is a place for one set of people, and a different place for others. The reader is positioned with the cartographer—we are new to the dialect and at a disadvantage when compared with the local speaker. Patterns of colonial power are overturned—there is a place we should not go or know. The presence of the dialect addresses a lack of representation in artforms that are typically reserved for European traditions. Miller's work confronts the notion that one voice has a greater right to representation in art than another.

Pasifika poets are making the same headway in New Zealand literature. The use of Samoan English in Tusiata Avia's poem 'Ode to da life' immediately establishes a perspective: the speaker is Samoan and imagines life after emigration as carefree:

> An all da Palagi dey very happy to us
> Dey say Hey come over here to Niu Sila
> Come an live wif us an eat da ice cream
> An watch TV2 evry day[14]

The irony is that this vision contrasts sharply with what follows in the collection. The cultural transition and reality of life in New Zealand is much more difficult. Through the presentation of dialect, poets like Avia and Miller are making the world hear a largely unheard voice. They offer the reader a different outlook, and they explore cultural tensions on the page.

It wanted to show you

We don't always have a positive reaction to the things we hear. Speech can be amusing, intriguing or reassuring, but sometimes it's flat-out offensive or upsetting. American poet Claudia Rankine responds to dialogue of this nature in her work.

In collaboration with her husband, filmmaker John Lucas, Rankine has created scripts to accompany videos, which appear in her collection *Citizen: An American lyric*. In one script Rankine uses only quotes from CNN news reports on the aftermath of Hurricane Katrina to create an entirely new work. The lines are both catalyst and content, and the result is a devastating text. Her arrangement serves to highlight the lack of assistance provided to victims of the hurricane. A significant number of these victims were African American, and on a larger level the poem addresses the invisibility of the black body.[15]

He said, I don't know what the water wanted. It wanted to show you no one would come.[16]

Rankine was incensed by the news reports she heard. These texts are her means of reply and a way to challenge injustice.

And yet, despite the emotional charge, her poems are controlled. How does she keep her composure and provide a measured response? Going back to what I heard on the bus, the dialogue wasn't offensive, but it pushed a button in me. The word 'costume' brought with it connotations of artifice. When I sat down to write a poem, the line became a real-world way to discuss larger problems that concern me about the current trajectory of global food production. Imagine a world where a butcher's shop is a literal front, erected to make consumers feel better about the fact that meat is now produced in a lab, a world where butchers are actors. A convincing red stain is specially formulated for the industry to be squirted onto aprons or spritzed on artificial meat. Using the dialogue in its original form kept the poem grounded. It prevented me from becoming too lofty or preachy, which is a natural urge when addressing a passionate topic. I found that sometimes the easiest way to tackle larger issues is to use smaller pieces.

In other words, why discuss what's troubling when you can simply show it? The product is infinitely more powerful. But Rankine hopes the chain reaction will not stop at her. The dialogue is not art in a static sense; it's not just to be looked upon. This is art that provokes its audience—she wants to generate action through her texts. 'It's time to be angry,' she says. 'It's time to say enough is enough.'[17]

This collection contains some of the most direct and disturbing poetry I have ever encountered—disturbing because it is the world reflected back at me, and I do not like what I see. In another section she presents a real-life exchange:

At the end of a brief phone conversation, you tell the manager you are speaking with that you will come by his office to sign the form. When you arrive and announce yourself, he blurts out, I didn't know you were black!

I didn't mean to say that, he then says.

Aloud, you say.

What? he asks.

You didn't mean to say that aloud.

Your transaction goes swiftly after that.[18]

As a citizen of the world, I felt shame when I read these poems. I began to analyse my own actions and behaviours, terrified I may find micro-aggressions that contribute towards prejudice and racism in New Zealand. Whatever I found I would be willing to acknowledge and change. I was not engaged; I was engulfed.

You're the only one I can talk to

When I first began to see my world in poetry, it had a lot to do with the use of speech. Poets like Jenny Bornholdt, Geoff Cochrane, James Brown and Kate Camp presented the kind of dialogue I both used and heard. It felt accessible. In Bornholdt's poem 'Then Murray Came', Murray arrives and says, 'I was sure you were having me on.'[19] I understand the kind of character Murray is because I am able to apply my own real-world local knowledge. Murray sounds like my uncle, my neighbour. He's a straight-shooter, a 'Kiwi bloke'. Murray is someone you can trust.

Most people I know don't read poetry, ever. They read novels and newspapers, watch films and they love music, but they won't go near poems for pleasure: they don't even consider it. I ask my friends why they don't read poetry and they say things like 'It's too difficult' and 'I don't know how'. Yet I am often asked to read poems at their weddings, or suggest a suitable poem for a funeral. It's strange that these people who feel they can't connect to the form still recognise that one of its strengths is interpreting the world around us. I consider that busload of young, enthusiastic people and what their world might be made of. Can they hear their voice in New Zealand poetry? I think there is much new New Zealand poetry that a modern audience would like and would be able to see themselves in.

Zarah Butcher-McGunnigle offers entry for an uncertain reader through 'everyday' dialogue in her 2014 debut, *Autobiography of a Marguerite*. But the dialogue also allows her to show the contrast between the mother and the narrator's understandings—it highlights their disconnect:

> She says, You're the only one I can talk to, the only one who will actually listen to
> me. Not chicken again, I think. I feel as though we had chicken yesterday and the
> day before, and the day before that, and the day before that.[20]

The language provides a level of comfort to the reader that permits
Butcher-McGunnigle to challenge them. She makes the ordinary exciting by
pushing at the boundaries of what poetry can be. She presents speech in new
and stimulating ways, using form to further communicate meaning. There is
no punctuation or line breaks to indicate dialogue. Although attributives
assist, we must accustom ourselves to the characters' voices in order to
differentiate the mother's speech from the narrator's thoughts.

> It's not dinner time yet, but there's nothing else to do. What do you want for dinner,
> my mother asks. I'm sitting at the table, closed, refrigerated. We'll have chicken, she
> says. The chicken has been defrosting for hours in the sink. She takes out baby
> carrots and baby leeks. I always wanted more babies, at least one more, but I
> couldn't because of your father. He never gave me any support with you and your
> sister. I had to do everything, he worked such long hours, he always went away for
> the weekend, he always did exactly what he wanted to do, oh, what's changed. I
> don't say anything.[21]

This is clever construction. Identities blur, but we also see less of the poet's
hand than what is usually exposed by formatting—we get closer to the
subjects themselves. The embedded dialogue reflects the narrator's struggle
to differentiate herself from her mother. Butcher-McGunnigle is attracted to
the speech she hears around her, but is also able to recognise it as an effective
writing tool and use it to her advantage.

I love the unimportant thing

> But my whole pleasure is the inconspicuous;
> I love the unimportant thing.[22]

Writers know how valuable the 'unimportant thing' can be—they hunt it. I
continue to ride buses I don't usually catch. I try to remain alert: at the cricket,
in a cinema or supermarket, my dialogue-harpoon at the ready. I like to go to
galleries and half-look at paintings, hoping to hear a snippet of conversation
I can use. I am struck by the things I hear people say, because they are often
more fantastic than what my imagination might allow. It would never have

occurred to me to use the word 'costume' in place of 'uniform'. It was like some kind of wonderful short-circuit. I could already see the speaker's boyfriend in my mind—donning his black and white striped apron with pride and a flourish, ready to perform.

What I had heard was electric and I wanted to harness that. Poems that incorporate found speech are accessible, but not simple. They function on a number of levels; they are lush and diverse. Bringing collected speech into our poems may be one of the most powerful ways we have to get people reading, enjoying and engaging with poetry—getting the world into poetry to get the world into poetry.

Notes

1. See http://officialharvarduniversity.tumblr.com/post/116090659913/i-dont-know-how-i-got-here
2. See www.facebook.com/overheardwholefoods
3. See http://paperspast.natlib.govt.nz/cgi-bin/paperspast?a=d&d=TS18850905.2.20.3 &e=
4. See www.judithhenry.net/theme/projects/overheard-book-series-2/
5. Bill Bell, 'Drop her a line anytime', *New York Daily News*, 7 August 2007.
6. Mary Wollstonecraft Shelley, *Frankenstein: Or, the Modern Prometheus* (Henry Colburn and Richard Bentley, 1831), x.
7. Ibid., xii.
8. See www.bbc.co.uk/programmes/articles/41rDvmTW0T1JWjXkcvZtMqt/about
9. Jenny Bornholdt, 'Photograph', *Best New Zealand Poems 2005*: www.victoria.ac.nz/modernletters/bnzp/2005/bornholdt.htm. As Bornholdt explains in the accompanying note to the poem, the lines are directions from the photographer who was arranging the 2003 New Zealand Arts Foundation laureates in position.
10. Andrew Johnston and Bill Manhire, 'Afterword: An email interview with Andrew Johnston', in *Doubtful Sounds: Essays and interviews* (Wellington: Victoria University Press, 2000), 283.
11. Glen Colquhoun, 'Aunty Flu', *The Art of Walking Upright* (Wellington: Steele Roberts, 1999), 61.
12. William Letford, 'Wit is it', *Bevel* (Manchester: Carcanet, 2012), 17.
13. Kei Miller, 'x. in which the cartographer asks for directions', *The Cartographer Tries to Map a Way to Zion* (Manchester: Carcanet, 2014), 27.
14. Tusiata Avia, 'Ode to da life', *Wild Dogs Under My Skirt* (Wellington: Victoria University Press, 2004), 25.
15. Rankine often speaks of this. See the interview in BOMB 129: http://bombmagazine.org/article/10096/claudia-rankine

16. Claudia Rankine, 'August 29, 2005/Hurricane Katrina' (script for Situation video), *Citizen: An American lyric* (Graywolf Press, 2014), 85.
17. These quotes taken from a television interview on Tavis Smiley, 8 December 2014.
18. Claudia Rankine, *Citizen: An American lyric*, 44.
19. Jenny Bornholdt, 'Then Murray Came', *How We Met* (Wellington: Victoria University Press, 1995), 66.
20. Zarah Butcher-McGunnigle, *Autobiography of Marguerite* (Auckland: Hue & Cry Press, 2014), 24.
21. Ibid.
22. Bill Manhire, 'Milky Way Bar', *Milky Way Bar* (Wellington: Victoria University Press, 1991), 19.

Nicole Page-Smith, 'Untitled', 2008.

THERESE LLOYD

There's probably a pill for this: An essay on addiction

Our family's doctor was bearable only with a large dose of black humour. We used to joke that if you went to see Dr Tolley with a sore right arm, you'd come out in much the same state, but with a mysterious new pain in your left arm. When I think of him, I think of iron. Grey, sharp and cold. His instruments were cold and his office was permanently in shade. The room smelt like cold air and dust. The items on his desk, which I can picture with alarming clarity, carried a similar sense of steely gloom: two fountain pens pointing out at aggressive angles from a plastic holder, his name in white letters on a black strip mounted on a wooden block. Black jellybeans in a lidless jar, a pale green light illuminating a small recess for a basin where he'd aggressively wash his hands.

As a kid I suffered from a lot of ear infections that caused me a great deal of anguish. I remember describing the pain to my mother once as an army of ants marching in an endless line, stomping their heavy boots. I can still see the image that my five-year-old self created—ants in combat gear and helmets booming and thundering ad infinitum.

Even as a child, when visiting Dr Tolley, I could sense that he would sooner be doing something else. Maybe that's why he pushed the otoscope so hard into my ear, and placed the tongue depressor so far down my throat I'd gag each time. There was certainly a touch of the sadist in Dr Tolley; or, at best, he was heavy handed.

Perhaps it's just the acuteness of these memories that make me feel as if I was always at his clinic, or perhaps it was that, as the youngest child out of five, with all my siblings off at school, I accompanied my mother everywhere, and she seemed to go to the doctor's a lot.

★

Substance abuse and addiction tend to announce themselves sooner or later, and often in catastrophic ways. Some addictions, however, are more insidious than others. My mother suffers from two of them: food and prescription medication.

My mother's relationship with food has always been a complex one. When I was growing up, her life seemed to revolve around a dazzling plethora of fad diets. Ridiculous and comical diets like the Israeli Army Diet, which consisted of two days eating only apples, two days of cheese, and two days of boiled chicken. Or the Hip and Thigh Diet, which promised you could 'spot shrink' pounds off those particularly meaty areas of your body. There were various drink powders that made bland murky shakes, the Grapefruit Diet, the Little and Often Diet, Weight Watchers, and many more. Mercifully, these days, informed discussion aided by sound scientific research shows that dieting seldom achieves its desired end. In fact, it is often the cause of weight gain. But the proliferation of fad diets shows no sign of diminishing and neither does my mother's unyielding belief that reaching her ideal weight is just a matter of finding the right diet.

When her efforts to lose weight failed, as they were bound to, my mother sought help from Dr Tolley. He prescribed her Desoxyn, a drug that was given, at that time, primarily to suppress appetite, but one that also carries a carpetbag of side-effects, including anxiety, migraines and insomnia. The street name for this drug is speed, and anyone who's taken it recreationally will tell you that long-term daily ingestion first thing in the morning before you drop the kids off to school is probably not ideal.

Recently my mother told me it had never crossed her mind to take medication for her weight. She said that during an appointment with Dr Tolley for something else entirely he remarked, 'So, Margaret, your weight— you don't care that you're the size of a house?' It's hard to fathom a doctor saying something like that, even one like Dr Tolley whose bedside manner consisted of a slap on the arse, and these days I've grown accustomed to taking generous pinches of salt with my mother's recollections. But whatever the case, speed was prescribed and speed was what she did. Very soon, Margaret became Super Margaret. Now she had the energy to look after her five kids, manage her erratic alcoholic husband, and eventually work full time as well.

The weight fell off her and for most of the 1980s she remained at an average weight for a woman of her small stature. The visible and immediate effects of taking prescription drugs were new to my mother and ultimately brought about a fundamental shift in her attitude towards medicine. Up until then she had approached illness and pain with a kind of Presbyterian stoicism—headaches were fixed with a couple of Disprin and stomachaches with Schweppes ginger ale. But if simply taking a pill could achieve the one thing she'd struggled with in vain for many years, and enable her to lose weight without the effort of dieting and its attendant guilt and shame, the question had to be asked: what other things could pills do?

*

It was 1986 when my parents packed up those of us still living at home in Napier to start a new life in Christchurch. For reasons unknown to me at the time, my father decided that all his problems (while I didn't know what they were, I knew there were many) could be solved by a massive relocation. New city, new job, new house, new life. These sorts of overhauls were reasonably common in our household, so much so that we jokingly gave the phenomenon its own name, 'New Regime'.

My mum took her own addictions with her to Christchurch, far less visible than my father's alcoholism. For a long time I denied the possibility that food could be addictive; I mean, it's a necessity, after all. So many aspects of our lives are geared towards the preparing, eating and sharing of food, particularly so when there's a large brood to be fed. For me, food preparation and the gifting of baked goods remains one of the principle pleasures in life. One of my favourite baking recipe books is Alexa Johnson's *Ladies a Plate*, not just for her traditional and unashamedly patriotic recipes, but for her nostalgic recollections of baking with her mother. The tender descriptions of recipes carefully modified over years, and passed between women from one generation to the next. I've been known to cry at these descriptions, and have written more than a few poems in response:

Small Depression

It broke like a teardrop
in a bowl of flour
sinking down to form
the beginnings of a crumble

My mother was a simple yet perfect baker. Her jam kisses in particular I remember with awe. Pale yellow and light as air with a not-too-sweet finish and delicate crust. I've never been able to achieve the same masterful results. Her sultana cake was sublime; although, since becoming a proficient baker myself, I've found that most things are delicious when you throw a pound of butter at them.

In more recent years when Mum started to decline in both physical and mental health, I would remind her of her former baking triumphs as a way to buoy her up. I'd suggest to her that she bake a banana cake to take to her friend's wedding anniversary, or some ginger crunch to take to her sister's house at Easter. She never took up my suggestions. The furthest she ever got was to buy expensive cake tins from Ballantynes that she didn't need, to transport the imagined baked item.

*

In Christchurch things went from bad to worse. This is a common trajectory in the lives of untreated addicts—and, by association, their families. Trying to manage my father's impetuousness proved a job too big for my mother. Before the first year was up, he'd decided that his new job was 'untenable'. My mother panicked. Apparently the best job he'd ever had—company car, expense account, tremendous salary—and he chose to pack it in because he decided his boss was a 'posturing dilettante'. Always a worrier, Mum found she couldn't sleep with the stress of it all. A few days of anxiety-induced insomnia ensued before she remembered, 'There's probably a pill for this.' She was prescribed with Triazolam, a sedative under the class of benzodiazepines, affectionately known as benzos—a short course for 14 days, to help her resume a normal sleep pattern. That was 26 years ago, and she's been taking benzos in one form or another in increasing doses ever since.

Luckily for her—and indeed her family—she hadn't been able to find a doctor in Christchurch who would prescribe her Desoxyn, so at least the benzos weren't in a precarious stand-off with adrenalin-pumping speed. But as the years wore on and her dosage increased, the soporific effect of the benzos crept into her waking hours, often leaving her in a mild state of semi-catatonia, unable to do much more than eat and watch TV.

It was around this time that pills became her first and only recourse for any ailment, large or small. Before long, she had both a morning and evening ritual of dosing up on at least 20 different medications, the function of some of which she could no longer recall. But even more alarming than her physical decline was her change in attitude. While one could not say that Mum's outlook on life had ever been overly optimistic, now it was subsumed by an unshakable resentment toward everyone and everything. None of this I recognized; none of this made sense to me. There is no doubt that being married to an alcoholic takes an enormous toll on a person's life. Sometimes they don't come back. Sometimes they withdraw so far into themselves that their own personal recovery seems impossible. This is true of my mother. But the combination of being married to an alcoholic and her own quietly raging addictions curdled in a toxic brew of depression, anger and victim mentality.

★

My mother. I love her because when I was young she was kind and gentle. Her short stature belied her undeniable strength. It's easy to forget—now that her addictions have led to her physical incapacity—that she raised and cared so beautifully for five small children. That she'd scoop us up and swing us around. That when I was very small, she'd play endless repeats of 'Where's Therese?', when I'd hide under the sheets as she attempted to make all the beds in the house.

Whether or not my mother was conscious of this, she stumbled upon a powerful method of combating my father's unruliness. She simply used food and drugs to cope with his drinking. The result was a stunning battle between two self-destructive wills. When he would drink, she would eat or pop pills. When he would gamble, she would buy makeup and clothes. When he did anything self-centred, foolhardy, or reactive, she would respond in kind.

How does a strategy like this pan out? The ethos of support groups for people whose lives have been affected by living with an alcoholic is to turn the focus away from the alcoholic and towards yourself. You're encouraged to understand that you didn't cause their addiction, nor can you control it, nor can you cure it. The non-alcoholic becomes empowered to live a full and productive life, whether or not the alcoholic is still in it. At the heart of these support groups is acceptance—not of a life of drudgery and degradation— but of the fact that alcoholism is bigger than any individual, including the alcoholic, and certainly bigger than all who are sucked into its vortex. I wish Mum had known about such support groups when we were growing up. They might have helped her to come up with a different strategy to the one she fell into.

Without speed, Mum's weight ballooned, and the cycle of fad diets began again. I can't recall the exact time she started to blame her spiral of weight gain and addiction on me, but I believe it was sometime at the start of the millennium. Mum's new favourite pastime was to sit in her chair at home and bitterly flick through her mental address book seeking, and usually finding, people to blame for what she considered to be her terrible lot in life. My father, naturally, was the primary offender, but all of my siblings copped it at one point or another. However, as Mum has reminded me on many occasions, her addiction to prescription drugs only began when she couldn't shift the weight she gained after her last child was born in 1974. That was me.

★

Blame is a fascinating phenomenon. It's a bit like drinking a cup of lethal poison in the hope that it will kill your enemy. Slowly but surely, the more you indulge in the blame game, the more it becomes the only plausible and rational way to explain your personal shortcomings. It's not my fault, he/she/ society did it. There's no question that I indulged in this game myself, blaming my parents for all the things I deemed unpalatable in my own life. Perhaps this is just the rite of passage of any child. Or perhaps this was some kind of learned behaviour, modelled by parents whose lives were ruled by powerful addictions that had tricked them into believing they were benign.

I've spent most of my life wanting my mother to change. When I was a kid,

I wanted her to be happy, but that came from a place of innocence and concern, the kind that is common to children. When I was a teenager, I wanted her to be cooler. I wished she'd wear stylish clothes, listen to better music, leave my dad, get a life. Since then it's been a blend of wishing that she cared more about others, as well as wishing she'd eat properly, quit the pills, go to rehab, start exercising, stop being a snob, stop watching so much TV, stop spending money as if she had any, stop calling Ballantynes 'Ballies', start doing some housework, become a volunteer, be involved in her grandchildren's lives, and stop telling herself that she's Lady Slane from Vita Sackville-West's *All Passions Spent*. And make no mistake, these have not been silent wishes. Every one of the above I've harped on about to her repeatedly, for years.

I've used stories of my mother's sometimes shocking behaviour and poor health as joke fodder in many conversations with friends. I used to refer to her as Moby, or 'the great whale'. I would regale my friends with humorous yarns about poorly timed flatulence in airports, or having to hoist her waterlogged leg into the car, and how the car listed distinctly to the left as we groaned down the road. Or the infamous Mother's Day when my sister called her and said, 'Happy Mother's Day, Mum!', to which Mum hissed in darkly bitter tones, 'Is it?'

★

The year I turned 39, a whole lot of change happened in my life: my marriage ended, I started a PhD, and Mum relocated from Christchurch to Martinborough, an hour's drive from where I live. As that tumultuous year wore on, I became overwhelmed by what felt like forces beyond my control. It was in this same difficult year I discovered meditation (as opposed to medication!). Meditation has been nothing less than transformative. I am a regular practitioner of this thing that I cannot claim to understand or even do very well. But I meditate every day, and have done so now for close to two years, sometimes with a specific thought or person in mind, sometimes a concept such as compassion. Sometimes I just focus on my breath and hope for the best. Meditation has helped me in ways that feel too nebulous and airy-fairy to describe. Words like presence, space, calm and serenity all spring to mind, and yet none of them feels exactly right. All I can say is that since trying to adopt an attitude of mindfulness through the regular practice of meditation, I feel better.

Inexplicably, in that difficult year, as I shuffled from one drama to the next, while still maintaining a regular meditation practice, I felt a change in attitude towards my mother. Randomly, a memory would float back to me: Mum giving me an eggcup with little rectangular chocolate chips in it when I was sick as a child. I remember picking at them, carefully eating one at a time until my fingers were smeary with chocolate. Another memory of nestling into the square space made by her bent legs on the couch, my arm draped over her waist. Or the time she stayed up late making two dozen delicate butterfly cakes, dollop of jam, cream, wings and all, for me to take to the school gala, only to discover that I'd given her the wrong date and the gala was in a week's time.

★

What brings about forgiveness in a person where beforehand there had only been resentment? My mum has said many hurtful things to me over the years, often reinforcing my sense that she regretted having children and that we'd all ruined her life. One of them was, 'I regret having had so many children; you've all ruined my life.' Or there's the oft-repeated one that questions my sheer existence. I'm the youngest out of five, and while all my siblings are roughly a year apart, there's a conspicuously longer gap of about five years before I came along. Repeatedly having your name and the word 'mistake' used in the same sentence becomes wearying after a while. Or there was the time Mum told me when I was a teenager that if I wanted more friends, I'd need to lose 5 kg. It's beside the point, but I was kind of skinny. A more recent barb was during a return trip to Martinborough and as we passed the pub in Featherston, Mum said, 'Oh come on, let's stop off for a glass of wine. You were much more interesting when you were drinking anyway.' I'd just the month before told her I'd quit drinking.

The litany of less-than-supportive things that Mum has said to my siblings and me over the years would make for dreary reading, and a dreary experience in writing it too. So let's leave it with those few examples and assume you can fill in the blanks.

*

Attending to the present moment means that whatever is in front of you is what you have to grace with a mindful awareness. Whether that's brushing your teeth, eating a piece of toast, typing an email, or spending time with your mother. Whatever it is, is all there is. The curious thing about practising mindfulness is that you start to notice more. And I'm not just talking about things in nature like, 'Oh wow, I've never seen the variegations of green on that flax bush before' (although that can happen too). It's as though a space grows around your comprehension of thoughts, feelings and ideas. A sort of stereoscopic view unfolds that enables you to see things less superficially, and from alternative angles. Like I say, it's hard to describe.

When I was driving Mum back and forth between Martinborough and Wellington hospital after a recent medical issue, I was struck by how much compassion I felt for her. Up until then, all I could see was a woman whose hedonistic lifestyle of pill popping and binge eating had left her physically incapacitated, morbidly obese, addicted, and mean as a snake. But as I pushed her around the hospital in a wheelchair, and helped her in and out of beds and chairs, I felt a tenderness for her that I haven't felt since I was a kid; since drinking tea and watching re-runs of Mary Tyler Moore with her after school, or the time she came with me to hear Lauris Edmond read poetry at the Christchurch Repertory Theatre when I was a teen.

*

I forgive my mother her hurtful comments and I hope that one day she will forgive me mine. Some of her decisions about how to live her life have been poor, but poor decision-making skills are not enough reason to condemn a person forever more. (I say this partly in hope, having made a number of tremendous blunders throughout my own short life.) And ultimately, they are her decisions.

I can make my own. I can choose not to let the same stripe of bitterness that's coloured much of these past 26 or so years for her, leaving her sick and resentful, colour my own. Or I can choose to see it differently. I can choose to remember the upsetting things she's said, or I can remember the loving, affectionate and intelligent woman that I knew as a child. Is this just a case of selective memory? Cherry-picking the sweeter moments and ignoring the swampy roots and broken branches? Yes, possibly. But is that so wrong? The problem with focusing on the negative aspects of a person's life is that, like blame and wanting someone else to change, it's highly addictive. I've often found myself ruminating on memories of my mother, looking for the bits that hurt the most, sometimes even looking to stories from her own childhood to find evidence to prove she's always been this way. But ultimately, this pursuit leads to misery for the pursuer, tainting whatever is good, and creating a skewed version of everything else.

Forgiveness may be something that can be manufactured, drummed up out of a sense of urgency or need. But in my experience, it has happened seemingly beyond my awareness. Meditation has somehow enabled me to get in touch with something bigger than the rawness of hurt feelings and bruised ego. It has created a mental space of refuge that I can visit whenever I need to. No pill necessary.

I have no way of knowing whether the next barbed comment from Mum won't catapult me into my old ways of blaming and judging. But I do know that by attempting to be mindful, attentive to the moment, and maintaining a compassionate heart to the best of my abilities, I stand a much better chance of seeing the goodness that has always been the essence of my mum; of all of us in fact.

ALAN RODDICK

Farthest South with Dr Sparrman

(Anders Sparrman, 1748–1820)

1. *Autumn, 1757*

A-one and a-two and a-hup,
and he's off,

perched on the tailboard
backwards, to wave

to his Mother, wrapped
in the arms of her children

outside his Father's church
this fine September morning.

The cart lurches, and he hangs on
for the longest journey of his life,

Tensta Village to Uppsala,
half a day. Nine years old,

and he's off to university,
his Father behind him

discussing the harvest.
He settles in, one arm across

the cabin trunk packed with his clothing,
washed, mended, labelled by his Mother,

and a letter in his Father's hand
addressed to one 'Dr Linnaeus'.

His fingers burnish the metal studs
that spell his name: SPARRMAN. Already

Tensta is gone. He kicks his heels
to spur on the travelling world.

2. *To the Children of the Dutch Resident,*
False Bay, Cape Province
21st November 1772

Dear Children, when you read these words
I shall have sailed with Captain Cook
on his voyage to discover
that Unknown Southern Continent.

I have told you about this
Terra Australis Incognita,
Land of Ice, or Pearls—or Nutmeg,
they say; but people say what they want.

I shall meet the Ruler of that land
to tell him of his nearest neighbours,
my best pupils, the Dutch Resident's
children who live at False Bay.

He will hear of your collections,
your butterflies and wildflowers
organised scientifically,
as Dr Linnaeus taught me,

as I have taught, and you have learned.
When your new tutor arrives,
teach him what you have learned from me.
It is right that the student

should then become the teacher.
When you are older, you too
may go exploring as I have done,
in Africa, to China—who knows where!

But we need not travel, to explore.
Just look around you, my Master said.
Good counsel for you, as it is for me,
your devoted tutor, Anders Sparrman.

3. *The Experimental Gentlemen*
14th December 1772

From Sixty North to Sixty South,
Tensta in Sweden to this No-Where,
the world is turning upside down

where flightless birds fly underwater,
fish are shot as they swim by,
fresh water's hauled from the sea in creels,

mountains dissolve and islands float.
No new lands for Cook to chart, but
a world of interest for us—

the artists and astronomers
and botanists he calls his own
'Experimental Gentlemen'.

4. *Christmas Day, 1772*

Seeing that the People
(said the Captain)
were inclinable to celebrate
Christmas Day in their own way,
I brought the Sloops under a very snug sail
least I should be surprised
with a gale of wind   with a drunken crew.

Naked to the waist
in a midsummer snowfall,

they ride a sea-chest knee to knee
to knock each other senseless.

Bare knuckles cracked with frost
split open, as the ring

of shouting crewmen wavers about
the tilting deck. Bets are laid, and

rum rations hang on a lucky miss,
one lucky haymaker.

British savages
(said Dr Sparrman).
Few people in Sweden understand
the methods of boxing ...

Better that the crew
should settle disputes
for a more certain peace
by fighting (say the Officers).

Christmas. Savages. Peace.
Oceanic indifference
swallows their words.

5. *Landfall*
26th March 1773

After four months, three thousand leagues
of fruitless search for *imaginary Lands*
ice-blink, aurora, floating rocks,
where snow-capped mountains seen at sunset
vanish without name by sunrise:

To enter by gates of rock and birdsong
his *Dusky Baie*, where *we were all strangers*,
stepping carefully to the plummet's pluck
40 fathoms ... no ground with 60 ...
(the leadsman hardly believed his ears):

To port, one island where seals gazed
with wary interest from their haul-out rocks;
to starboard, shaped like a seaman's headgear
another island shaggy with woods,
a glory of bird-calls overhead.

By lamplight, Cook turned to charting
safe harbour on that remorseless shore,
fixing in ink their solid presence:
Nomans Island. Thrum Cap.
Stop Island. Prove Island. Anchor Point.

6. *Yesterday*
Saturday 27th March

Yesterday
Cook's *Resolution* delivered
artists, astronomers,
botanists and mapmakers,
rats and mice and,
thanks to Mr Harrison's watch,
a Friday in March
to Dusky Bay.

7. *First Ascent*
St George's Day, 1773

Botanists and navigators both
live by finding, and by naming—
Point Five Fingers, Doubtful Harbour.

Too late in the season for flowers,
ferns and lichens filled our herbarium
at the Forsters' lake and Luncheon Cove.

New Zealand woods did not welcome
their first overlords of Nature: each step
we hacked down ... scrambled under ...

climbed over ... creepers massing
to stop our advance and block retreat.
But botanists, like navigators

need horizons to chase, and here
all horizons were mountain tops.
With Mr Pickersgill then, map-maker,

and Master Gilbert from our sister ship,
I clambered with difficulty this day
to reach a high mountain summit

where I discovered one more new shrub
to name for my fellow botanist,
Forstera sedifolia.

Breathless we strode that horizon, between
a savage chaos of snow-topped ranges
and, snug at Astronomers Point, our ship,

her longboat making for Sportsman Cove.
To celebrate St George's Day
we set fire to dry grass on the peak.

The fire took hold and spread, to make
a fine show when at sunset, our Captain
charted one more name: Mt Sparrman.

8. Thus Far, and No Farther!
30th January 1774

Fifty more days and nights for the crew,
aloft in hailstorms to shorten sail,

the ropes like wires, sails like board,
sheaves in their blocks encased in ice,

Tahiti no more than a hot memory,
a bright dream at any hint of northing.

This day brought *an immence Ice field ...*
Ninety Seven Ice Hills or Mountains ...

vastly large ... two hundred feet high ...
we could not proceed One inch farther South ...

I was not sorry, said Cook, at meeting
with this interruption. — *But Ne plus ultra!*

young midshipman Vancouver shouted,
inching out along the bowsprit

as the crew prepared to tack about.
Did Sparrman see Vancouver's triumph?

To avoid the bustle and crowd, he wrote,
I went below to my cabin to watch ...

the boundless expanses of Polar ice.
Thus it happened, as my companions observed,

that I went a trifle farther south
than any of the others ... because a ship,

when going about ... has a little stern way
before the fresh tack when the sails fill.

Backwards into history then
our Experimental Gentleman.

FIONA KIDMAN

Our Young Selves

At the end of the conference today
I am standing in a white hotel room:
yes, that sounds like the title of a novel
my friends and I admired years ago.
So many hotel rooms, so much
baggage I've carried in and out

of them. This one is more crowded
than usual. I am on the fourth floor
looking across a lake that is turning
purple in the dusk, an island dark
at its centre. This is a scene
I have described a score or more

times. There are also two
people inhabiting it, they are
sitting on the steps of a low
house with pale stucco walls
and a verandah running across
its width. The girl is just out
of her teens, the man somewhat

older, though you would not think
so to look at him. The dishes are still
on the table, in the background Nat King
Cole sings 'Unforgettable', soon
as night settles in they will stand,
perhaps waltz once or twice
around the sitting room

as he leads her towards the bedroom.
Oh, these people are characters in a story
book, they have yet to go through serial
crime, whodunits and why, true romance,
all the pulp fiction you could ever
imagine. What lies beneath me
this evening is a row of motels

and neon lights where the stucco
house with the verandah once
stood, the young couple long
gone on their way. And yet.
And yet what, you might ask? It's
just that, in this gathering darkness,
there appear to be two elderly
people walking hand in hand
in a resolute way along the edge
of the lake, remembering their lines.

MICHAEL HARLOW

A Small Magnificence, Just Buzz Me Miss Blue

'In all honesty, I find it magnificent when a solitary woman walks down a green avenue', making conversation with herself, plucking invisibles from the air: *He loves me, he loves me not, he loves me* ... More than a mere parcel of words she has been carting about emptying them here and there. No, she is always on the alert for the right time the right place to let them fly, and see what they discover. 'Just buzz me Miss Blue', she replies to all the ordinary questions that swarm around her. Flurries of birdsong that follow her. The noise of yellow flowers opening. The pigeon-flying clouds she reads with riddling regard.

Well, she's a Bag Lady, isn't she? And she's got to survive even herself, my friend says who hangs around Bryant Park by the library, snapping photos for an Album for Young Ladies from a Swiss finishing school. One of those 'lost' in order to be found again, isn't it?, he says.

In one of the photos, Miss Blue is there, a solitary figure; and he has caught her, with a wink of the eye, walking on cushions of air. It seems incredible, but sometimes the branched heart is the imagination itself, isn't it? Always, she is looking out for something to happen that might make a difference, *He loves me not, he loves me* ... And her heart hand busy darting on air: words want wings, don't they, they have to go somewhere.

And she recalls, once it was some words were sent as angels, she says. Long years and more, learning how to be ever alone with herself. 'Not all the pianos in the wood have power to mangle me,' she says. I can see that she knows something about dark hope. 'Just buzz me Miss Blue when you can,' is her reply.

JEFFREY HARRIS

EIGHT PAINTINGS

1. *Mother and Daughter at Okains Bay*, 1996–2015, 278 x 353 mm. Oil on board. Private collection, Christchurch.
2. *Magdalena at French Farm*, 1996–2012, 283 x 441 mm. Oil on board. Private collection, Sydney.
3. *Jillian and Calf at French Farm*, 1996–2012, 329 x 422 mm. Oil on board. Private collection, Doha.
4. *Anna*, 2013–15, 272 x 399 mm. Oil on board. Courtesy of Harris Smith Art, Dunedin.
5. *Jeremy*, 2013–15, 273 x 400 mm. Oil on board. Private collection, Auckland.
6. *Crucifixion 5*, 1997–2015, 331 x 201 mm. Oil on board. Courtesy of Harris Smith Art, Dunedin.
7. *Crucifixion 8*, 1997–2015, 331 x 205 mm. Oil on board. Courtesy of Harris Smith Art, Dunedin.
8. *Charlotte and Kevin at Okains Bay*, 1976–2014, 312 x 406 mm. Oil on board. Private collection, London.

These eight paintings are from the exhibition *Renaissance Days*, to be held at the Dunedin Public Art Gallery from 28 November 2015 to 20 March 2016. *Renaissance Days* is an exhibition of 22 oil paintings by Jeffrey Harris begun many years ago and completed between 2008 and 2015.

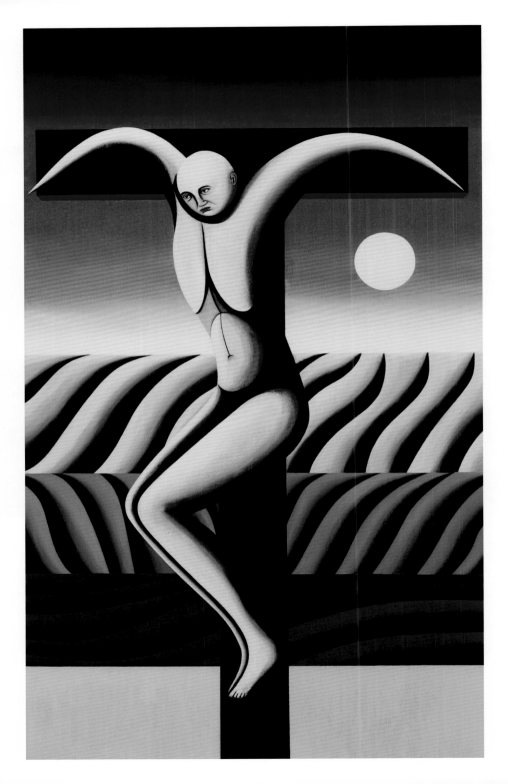

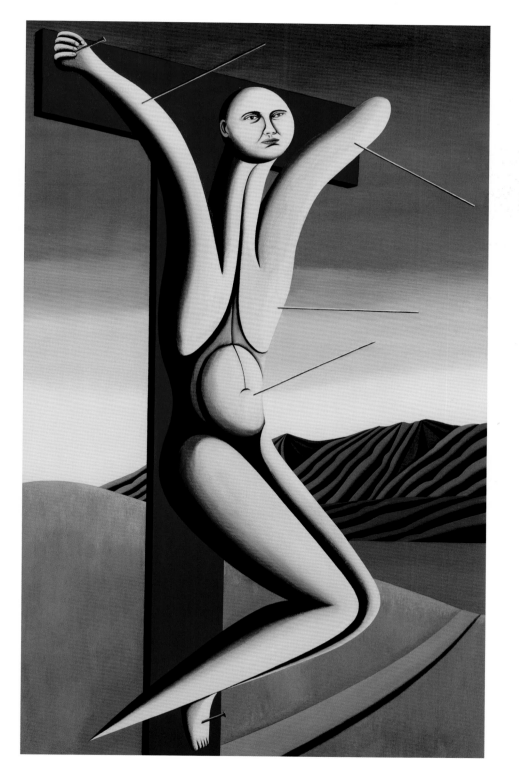

BERNADETTE HALL

The Parachutist

he's hanging there
he's turned it and himself somehow
so he's out in front of it
he's tilted out to the left away from it
it looks like a light bulb   like a bright mushroom
like a grandfather-clock face and he's the pendulum
he can see the wheat fields down there
the vents and tears
where the cut grain sweeps around small trees
the whisk that follows the whale boat
he's in love with them, the planet wanderers
so close their radiance passes through air
with scarcely a diversion
he's in love with Saturn with its rings of ice and dust and rock
he's in love with moon-white Venus
with the whole celestial puzzle (*fantastical nostrums of astrology*)
but most of all it's Earth that he's in love with
so lovely in her *sequestered circle*
she's the one that calls and calls and calls to him

ROBERT SULLIVAN

The Black River

i.
We have reached a black glass river
of faces sliding into the next, cracks
chipping ears, noses rubbed off

I would cross it but the sound
of bed socks on obsidian grates,
makes soft dots on black face boards

a domino river
sent spilling by whispering fingers ...
oh for a silent, steady hand

ii.
When I was younger and warmer
this river flowed like blood
we talked of punting at Oxford
and every smile held hope

but now I'm shivering
looking over the edge of my bed
into the black glass
as its fire dies

iii.
When the glass was hot
there was such fire!
Torrents geysers splashing
bright lakes of flame

with Mahuika's fingers
tapping the rim
for time

iv.
Her bright face was there
at the heart of the lake
te tau o taku ate

v.
I scrambled from the shore
doing my dog paddle
and my breaststroke
but she backstroked
and freestyled from me
to the horizon
in a sparkle
I was left here cooling
with the lake
looking for my pyjamas
with the polkadots
and my winter beanie

JOHN DENNISON

Hold

I am shaking all through; having descended (not lightly),
having descended at all it is surprising how,
ear-tumbled in the rusting air,
how still one is before the door.
Door which rises before all, and does
not now lift, which is breakwater and bow,
beyond which might be brightness flaring on the water,
(which is to say a gap unjumpable):
lift now, before we wonder at our predicament.
Above-decks was tea and bolted furniture,
and a weather charge across everything
as the ship shifted, slid in mid-strait
at the currents' crossing (stretch-marks on the belly
of the water). What is this predicament?
Great motives—yes—kick hard in the hold.
In the lee of the city, the tannoy calls it forth
from the congregating ship, wave
of unease, stream of bodies down the stair-
wells, unwondering at the whole shell
resounding with the bow-thrusters' scrummage,
a mind-scrubbing exuberation of steel
over the watery absolute. Light laughs
ugly in the hull, as trucks gather
darkness to their wheels, failed promise
of furthering and deliverance.
You are not to wonder at this nonchalance;
tremble with the rest, walnuts on the dash
before the shucking, as the ship racks itself
towards the wharf. That's the heart of it.
And still, the door.

CILLA McQUEEN

Power Riddle

Running free
or harboured in cells
not your cells
and not by bees
nor kept by keys
I sting quick as malice

I split trees
rock holds me to its heart
it queers the compass
I can make the sky explode
Interrupt me? Hah!
I'll give you lack.

Untree

And I was crushed in a hold.
I was lifted and blown into a mountain.

Drying, I came to my senses.
Machinery caressed me.

My unbeing slipped into a truck
that carried me to the slaughterhouse

Where I was zipped up and made whole.
My blood began to run.

They carried me to my dwelling
and placed me upright with blades.

Bike

Oh for a bike with rattly mudguards & a loose chain
with worn cotter pins & half-flat tyres & a wobbly carrier
with a cracked weather-worn leather seat & pedals that squeak
& a light that doesn't work with a dynamo that won't turn
a foot brake that only works when you back-pedal the rusty chain.

Give me a bike with black mudguards
with a stripe of white paint & a red reflector
a bike with high handle-bars & rubber grips & a loose front
brake with a frayed rusted cable
a bike with spokes missing & spokes bent from sticks & stuff
chucked up by trucks with a rear vision mirror clamped on
the front forks (so cool) so I can see what's coming behind
& pedal chasing dogs out of breath.

A bike with gears with racing handle-bars skinny tyres a bell
twelve-speed *deluxe*
a bike with a pouch with a puncture kit tucked behind the seat
for emergencies
(any old bike will do)
a flat road a gravel road a long road with a steep dip
to make my hair go flat & fast with dust & no brakes
with long cocksfoot grass racing past
a trip down memory lane.

I want a bike that'll do shortcuts across paddocks & won't get stuck
in muddy ruts
a bike that'll swerve cow-pats
& bump over rabbit holes without complaint

will lie in the thick long grass on a riverbank while I fish for trout
will be so old no one would want to steal it
will not care if I wander off leaving it there for the night
to be picked up next morning on my way to school.

I want a bike that'll fail the inspector's examination
bald tyres loose chain defective brakes dull reflector
no front brake perished pump leaky tube valves
a bike that knows its way around back roads
that can weave through a herd of slow-moving cows.

ANDY McKENZIE

The Last Circle

After the benediction, the last remaining senior members of the congregation of St Christopher's slowly descend the stairwell to the lounge for a cuppa, gathering in a semi-circle around a heater.

Marlys highlights her swollen legs, mentioning that her doctor is concerned about possible water retention, and that she feels like a junky because he's added yet another pill to her pill cocktail.

Audrey, whose shoulder was giving her hell and damnation last week, announces that she's found relief through a mobile Chinese herbalist and acupuncturist. She has his business card in her handbag if anyone would like his details.

Charlotte frowns, and warns Audrey about dabbling in Eastern spirituality, as it can be a gateway into the demonic; she heard this on the Bill Subritzky Hour on Radio Rhema.

Elsa says she saw Joyce Meyer on television this week, and thought she was fishy because she kept advertising her products and asking for donations. She adds that many televangelists are being investigated in the United States for tax evasion, fraud and money laundering; they're a pack of ferocious wolves disguised as sheep, she warns.

On the contrary, Marlys says, she likes Joyce Meyer—and Benny Hinn and Frank Hammond—and has no qualms, whatsoever, about donating a few pennies to their ministries. After all, they're reaching millions upon millions of lost souls for the Lord, which is more than she'll ever reach.

Bob says something, but since he's had a stroke he doesn't make a lot of sense, and Marlys turns, smiles, nods and pats his claw.

Vera avoids sitting opposite Bob, as looking at him makes her frightened— how one side of his face is drooping and trapped in a horrifying gaze; how he dribbles and blows bubbles from the corner of his mouth, and has to sip his coffee through a tube.

Charlotte shares that she's grateful to God because she's just received a letter confirming her hip operation in four months' time. However, she's trying not to be too hopeful, as this is the fifth letter she's received from the hospital, each time postponing her operation.

Elsa comments that won't it be grand when Jesus returns and we receive our resurrection bodies in a renewed heaven and earth. She quotes from the book of Revelation: 'He will wipe away every tear from their eyes. There will be no more death or mourning or crying or pain, for the old order of things has passed away.'

Audrey, like others in the group, finds some of Elsa's beliefs not quite evangelical, and says she's looking forward to floating off up to Glory, because she's tired and sore and had enough.

Most in the group nod.

Bob says something that nobody understands.

Vera congratulates Elsa on remembering her Bible so well, because she's been having memory lapses. Yesterday, for instance, she went out in her car, only to end up lost and disorientated, not knowing why or where she was going.

Audrey tells a sad story about an aunt who had dementia. She escaped from her residential care unit and was found drowned in a neighbouring goldfish pond.

When Charlotte and Marlys hear this they shudder, anxious that this could be their ending also, unless of course the Rapture occurs within the year, which is more than likely given what's going on in the Middle East.

Tessa, the pastor's wife, rolls up with the tea trolley enquiring if any in the group would like a top-up and another sample of Vera's delicious baking.

Vera looks surprised, and suggests that Tessa must be mistaken, as she has no recollection of doing any baking, let alone bringing any to church for morning tea.

Tessa laughs, telling her that there's only one Vera she knows, and pats her shoulder.

All get a top-up—including Bob—and add a piece or two of baking to their saucers.

Audrey compliments Vera on the moistness of her ginger and feijoa cake, and could she please bring a copy of the recipe along next Sunday so she could try baking it herself?

When Tessa wheels the tea trolley away, Vera becomes tearful and begins to heave and wail.

Simultaneously, Charlotte and Marlys pull handkerchiefs from down inside their bosoms and pass them over to Vera, assuring her that it'll be all right, just breathe through your nose and count backwards from twenty.

Bob begins to moan and blow bubbles, and Marlys, preoccupied with Vera, asks if Audrey would please reach over and pat Bob's claw until he quietens.

Charlotte leans forward and whispers that isn't Tessa looking dark-eyed and as thin as a willow branch, and that she'd heard from Katelyn, Pastor Dylan's part-time administrator, that something's wrong.

Adjusting her hearing aid, Elsa leans forward, hissing at Charlotte to stop gossiping; it's unchristian. However, adds Elsa, Charlotte is correct. Something is wrong with Tessa, as she's heard similar from Elliot, the session clerk, when he popped around with her annual offering receipt.

Vera, feeling a lot better, thank you, hands the handkerchiefs back and asks what all the whispering and askance glances are about.

Charlotte whispers into Vera's hearing aid that they're discussing what could be wrong with Tessa, as apparently something's not quite right with her.

Vera whispers back into Charlotte's whistling hearing aid that though she can't remember who exactly told her—perhaps Gale, the senior Sunday School teacher, or Trevor, the church's bookkeeper—that whatever's wrong with Tessa, it has something to do with her identity, whatever that means. Then again, Vera adds, she isn't exactly sure if it's Tessa having some sort of identity crisis or her neighbour Suzie, who suffers from bouts of misery and thrush. Or perhaps it's Beverley, her daughter's best friend, who's just discovered her husband has a thing for stockinged mannequins. Or perhaps … She starts to whimper and shake and tug at her freshly permed curls. She no longer knows who's connected to what, including herself.

Charlotte, her bifocals tracking Tessa's movements, whispers back to the group what Vera's just told her: that Tessa's having a crisis about her sexual identity. That she's discovered, after fifteen years of marriage and three lovely children, that she's a full-blown lesbian, for goodness sake!

Audrey splutters up her last mouthful of coffee, while Marlys nearly chokes on a bite of Vera's yummy walnut slice.

Bob jiggles his hips and thighs, and a pooey smell begins to emanate from around his seat.

Elsa sighs, reminding the group that St Christopher's can well do without another tragic drama. Their previous pastor, a South African import, impregnated their 22-year-old youth pastor and then whisked himself off with the church's entire savings and investments to a South Pacific atoll.

Marlys comments that if something like that happens again, it'll be the death of them.

And as the tea trolley squeaks by, they stare down at the crumbs in their laps, wondering who won't be here this time next week.

ROGELIO GUEDEA
(translated by Roger Hickin)

Three Poems

El oficio I
Las palabras no encuentran su habitación.
Pasan de una estancia a otra enredadas en una sábana blanca,
como la loca del pueblo.
Sólo les falta aullar.
Quiero decir que aúllan como las ambulancias
en las noches de la George Street.
Palidecen de insomnio.
Cambian intempestivamente los canales del televisor.
Comen pan duro: por desesperadas.
No estoy hablando del que escribe.
Yo no soy el que hace las metáforas del escribiente.
Estoy hablando de las palabras y su ejercicio de nacer.
De lo difícil que es verlas llegar a un país donde las demás palabras
conducen por la izquierda
y donde son realmente caros los abrigos de lana que podrían,
en todo caso, protegerlas del frío.

Vocation I
Words lack a room of their own.
They go from place to place
like the local madwoman, tangled in a white sheet.
All they want to do is howl.
And they howl like the ambulances
down on George Street at night.
They grow pale from insomnia.
They change the TV channel without warning.

Half starved they eat stale bread.
I'm not talking about someone who writes.
I'm not one of those hacks who makes up metaphors.
I'm talking of words and their efforts to be born.
Of how hard it is to see them arrive
in a country where the other words drive on the left,
of how expensive woollen coats are
that would protect them from the cold.

El oficio II

Esta mano, desde que aprendió a escribir, escribe tu nombre.
Lo pinta con letras grandes en las paredes del colegio.
O en la arena de la playa.
Lo escribe—tu nombre—con cincel o lápiz de punta fina: esta mano.
Esta mano, que se alarga hasta tocar una nube o un ala de pájaro,
desde que aprendió a decir, dice tu nombre.
Lo dice en las noches de frío, junto a la chimenea,
arropada con una frazada de lana, mientras escucha cantar a Amparo Montes.
Lo dice también bajo la lluvia: esta lluvia que la moja.
O de cara al viento: este viento que la lleva.
Esta mano sin brazo y sin hombro pero con ojos y boca,
desde que aprendió a recordar, te recuerda.
Su memoria es frágil como la tristeza del niño que no quiere ir a la escuela,
y que ahora está llorando escondido detrás del viejo sofá.
Es una mano sin memoria, entonces, pero esperanzada.
Esta mano, desde que aprendió a desear, te está deseando.
Es como si la llevara un pájaro hasta a ti.
No es un ruiseñor sino una torcacita.
No es un tren sino un avión sin paraderos.
Esta mano, desde que supo que existías, existe.
Trabajar, comer, andar las calles, dormir, leerte:
en todo eso se afana para decir tu nombre.
Tu nombre sin pasado ni futuro.
Este nombre de hoy que ha existido desde nunca y para siempre.

Vocation II

This hand, now it has learned to write, writes your name.
Paints it in big letters on the walls of the school.
Or in the sand at the beach.
Your name—it writes it with a chisel or a sharpened pencil: this hand.
This hand, that reaches up to touch a cloud or the wing of a bird,
now it has learned to speak, it speaks your name.
Speaks it on cold nights by the fire,
wrapped in a woollen blanket, listening to the songs of Amparo Montes.
And speaks it in the rain: this rain that soaks it.
Or into the wind: this wind that carries it.
This hand with no arm and no shoulder but with eyes and a mouth,
now it has learned to remember, it remembers you,
its memory fragile as the sadness of a child unwilling to go to school,
who cries now and hides behind the old sofa.
A hand, then, without memory, but hopeful.
This hand, since it learned to desire, is desiring you.
As if a bird had carried it to you.
Not a nightingale but a young wood pigeon.
Not a train but a plane with no place to land.
This hand, now it knows of your existence, exists.
To work, to eat, to walk the streets, to sleep, to read to you:
all these just to speak your name.
Your name without past or future.
This name now, since never, and a name for ever.

la casa sobre la espalda

escuchando hablar en la plaza comercial a gente del país extranjero,
riéndose del día nublado, sus relojes de pulsera recién
comprados, sus boinas mercenarias / no diciendo a nadie
el origen de esas manos que saludan o acarician,
ni el origen de esos pies que recorrieron kilómetros de odio
para llegar al país extranjero, ni el origen de esa boca que
no traicionó nunca a los desvalidos, ni el origen de esa
casa sin alas que lleva clavada con un clavo de dos pulgadas

en la espalda / mirando a su alrededor la gente que va
y que viene, los que van hacia el sur sin pasaporte
y los que vienen del norte, libres sus ojos de aduanas,
libres de celdas o puertas atrancadas / dándole nombre
falso al gendarme, al despachante de correos, al intendente
de la plaza comercial a donde va todos los días
a esperar a que se acabe el día, otro día más,
para empezar de nuevo.

his house on his back
listening in the mall to the talk of people of another country,
their laughter at the cloudy day, the wristwatches they've just
bought, the mercenaries' berets they're wearing / not telling anyone
where these hands are from that greet or caress,
where these feet are from that crossed kilometres of hatred
to reach a foreign land, or where this mouth is from
that never betrayed the powerless, or where this
house without wings is from he carries nailed to his back
with four-inch nails / looking around him at the people coming
and going, those who go south without passports
and those who come from the north, their eyes free of Customs,
free of cells and barred doors / giving a false name
to the police, to the post office clerk, to the manager
of the mall he comes to every day
to wait until the day is over, one more day,
to make a fresh start.

JACK ROSS

Is it Infrarreal or is it Memorex?
Robert Bolaño's *Savage Detectives* and the Eternal Avant-garde

Mexico City, July 1982

Someone had to call Ulises's mother, I mean it was the least we could do, but Jacinto didn't have the heart to tell her that her son had disappeared in Nicaragua ... just like Ambrose Bierce and the English poets who died in the Spanish Civil War and Pushkin, except that in Pushkin's case his wife, Pushkin's wife, I mean, was Reality, the Frenchman who killed Pushkin was the Contras, the snows of St Petersburg were the empty spaces Ulises Lima left in his wake, his lethargy, I mean, and his laziness and lack of common sense, and the seconds in the duel were Mexican Poetry or Latin American Poetry, which, in the form of the Solidarity Delegation, were silent witness to the death of one of the best poets of our day.

—Roberto Bolaño, *The Savage Detectives* (1998), p. 321.

*

Auckland, April 2006

Dear Leicester,

Not that I suppose you've been missing it exactly, but I thought you might like to hear some old-fashioned, Auckland-style literary goss about a few of your old friends.

So there we all were in the little art gallery in Northcote: comfy sofas, cushions, tables of wine and cheese. The plan was that we should each read for five minutes, then have an interval with music, then read again for another five minutes, then there would be an open mike (necessary to get funding for the gig, apparently).

In shambles Donald, just before the readings begin. He looks a bit pasty to me, and has obviously had quite a bit to drink. He asks if I can give his magazine a bit of a puff. I say of course, but suggest that he read a poem himself later on in the open mike (I'm pretty keen on some of the poems he's been writing recently). He likes the idea, and goes off to get some copies of the mag from Craig's car, which is parked nearby.

Meanwhile the reading begins: read read read, yawn yawn yawn. Then the interval. I talk to Craig, who says he hasn't seen Donald for some time, since he went off to look in the car, in fact, and is a little worried about him ('He was popping anti-depressants in the car, and he's been drinking all day, and he was in hospital this morning with some cuts he'd made on himself.') Ah.

*

Mexico City, May 1977

Our visceral realist activities after Ulises Lima and Arturo Belano left: automatic writing, exquisite corpses ... masturbatory writing (we wrote with the right hand and masturbated with the left, or vice versa if we were left-handed), madrigals, poem-novels, sonnets always ending with the same word, three-word messages written on walls ('This is it,' 'Laura, my love,' etc.), outrageous diaries, mail-poetry, projective verse, conversational poetry, antipoetry ... poems in hard-boiled prose (detective stories told with great economy, the last verse revealing the solution or not), parables, fables, theatre of the absurd, pop art, haikus ... desperado poetry (Western ballads), Georgian poetry, poetry of experience, beat poetry ... lettrist poetry, calligrams ... bloody poetry (three deaths at least), pornographic poetry (heterosexual, homosexual, or bisexual, with no relation to the poet's personal preference) ... We even put out a magazine ... We kept moving ... We kept moving ... We did what we could ... But nothing turned out right.
—Roberto Bolaño, *The Savage Detectives*, p. 196.

*

Auckland, April 2006

The reading recommences. The first two do their sets, the third begins ... I'm standing to one side when in comes Donald. He *does* have copies of the latest

Bread, but seems very unsteady on his feet. He comes up to me and asks if he can read. I suggest that I'd better do it for him, as he doesn't look like he's in very good shape. We're just discussing the matter when he starts to fall over, unfortunately on the bare feet of the wife of one of the more senior poets present, who is sitting right next to me.

'You just stood on my feet! I have a bad toe!'

'Sorry,' mutters Donald, 'Bad hip ...'

At this point he starts to go over again, and I grab him to try and steady him.

Suddenly the senior poet is on the scene. 'You just stood on my wife's foot! You should get out of here!'

Donald protests; organisers start to cluster around.

'This is a paid event ... You have to leave ...'

'I've paid already,' says Donald. 'I don't see why I should leave ...'

The senior poet seizes him and starts to thrust him towards the door. Donald resists. Others start to join in. 'What's going on?' says Hilda, as her interminably dull reading about an alcoholic failing to resist the booze meanders on ...

 ★

Mexico City, November 1975

... the night before, when there were just a few of us left, Ernesto San Epifanio had said that all literature could be classified as heterosexual, homosexual, or bisexual. Novels, in general, were heterosexual, whereas poetry was completely homosexual; I guess short stories were bisexual, although he didn't say so.

Within the vast ocean of poetry he identified various currents: faggots, queers, sissies, freaks, butches, fairies, nymphs, and philenes. But the two major currents were faggots and queers. Walt Whitman, for example, was a faggot poet, Pablo Neruda, a queer. William Blake was definitely a faggot. Octavio Paz was a queer, Borges was a philene, or in other words he might be a faggot one minute and simply asexual the next. Rubén Darío was a freak, in fact, the queen freak, the prototypical freak.

'In our language, of course,' he clarified. 'In the wider world the reigning freak is still Verlaine the Generous.'

—Roberto Bolaño, *The Savage Detectives*, p. 72.

★

Auckland, April 2006

The senior poet (to do him justice) is clearly experienced in such matters and by now has Donald all the way to the door. Jack stands there like a stuffed dummy thinking how unnecessary this all is and wishing they'd all stop fighting. Craig and the friend he came with are trying to drag Donald away. Various impotent attempts at a fist-fight between Donald and the senior poet. Shouts, curses ...

Suddenly a wine glass comes flying through the door (presumably thrown by Donald) and detonates in the middle of the floor, luckily touching no one.

'Shut the doors!' shouts my colleague Myra. 'That way they can't get back in ...'

By now the mayor of Northcote, who used to be a cop, has got stuck in. The organisers are ringing the police. The senior poet and various other bystanders come back in. Calm settles in again, as Hilda's dreary words continue (she's started again at the beginning, lest we should have missed any of her words of wisdom).

★

Mexico City, November 1975

At [Don Crispín Zamora's] request, I talked to him about visceral realism. After he'd made a few observations like 'realism is never visceral,' 'the visceral belongs to the oneiric world,' etc., which I found rather disconcerting, he theorized that we underprivileged youth were left with no alternative but the literary avant-garde. I asked him what exactly he meant by underprivileged. I'm hardly underprivileged. At least not by Mexico City standards. But then I thought about the tenement room Rosario was sharing with me and I wasn't so sure he was wrong. The problem with literature, like life, said Don Crispín, is that in the end people always turn into bastards.

—Roberto Bolaño, *The Savage Detectives*, pp. 101–02.

*

Auckland, April 2006

The senior poet's as happy as a dog with two tails. 'Didn't think I still had it in me ... He was soft ... took mercy on him, but I could have dropped him easily with a single punch ...' etc etc to anyone who'll listen.

Hoping that Donald & Craig & co have pissed off and driven away, I do my bit of the reading, though the audience has thinned considerably (and understandably) by this time. The broken glass is mopped up, (relative) peace is restored ...

And now the cops come driving up. 'Why have they brought them back here?' asks Hilda. Waves of rumour come and go among those of us who are still hanging around. It seems that the mayor pursued the malefactors in his car with a cellphone, directing the cops to intercept them, which finally took place in the park at Stokes Point.

Craig (as he tells me later) elected to take the heat while Donald and an even drunker member of the group took off to hide under the piles of the Harbour Bridge.

*

Mexico City, November 1975

... when I was in high school we had a teacher who claimed to know exactly what he would do if World War III broke out: go back to his hometown, because nothing ever happened there, probably a joke, I don't know, but in a way he was right, when the whole civilized world disappears Mexico will keep existing, when the planet vaporizes or disintegrates, Mexico will still be Mexico ...

—Roberto Bolaño, *The Savage Detectives*, pp. 171–72.

*

Auckland, April 2006

By now the organisers appear to have worked out that it's *my* friends who've caused all the ruckus, so I think it best to leave before the cops can start questioning me and demanding addresses. On the way out, though, I encounter Craig. The cops simply let him go, as he hasn't really done anything wrong. They seemed pretty bored with the whole business, in fact. The irony is that nothing would have happened if the mayor hadn't happened to be there, and hadn't happened to be an ex-cop …

But now comes the clincher. I write to the organisers next day apologising for the disruption of their event in such a non-North Shore sort of way (however much such things may go on in town … Donald was almost arrested for a similar glass-throwing incident at a launch a couple of months before … Why is it that drunks always want to throw things, and they always choose things made out of glass?). They reply pretty graciously that it wasn't my fault, and I suppose it wasn't, though I do feel a bit bad about it nevertheless. And then in comes Myra (this is in the office, at work).

We giggle. 'Well, that went well,' I say (I'd invited all my students, though luckily none of them came—just the usual culture-vultures).

'So,' she asks, 'what's all this stuff about [the senior poet]?'

'What stuff?' I reply. 'All I remember is him skiting about what a hard man he still is.'

'I've just been hearing that those friends of yours told the cops he'd been molesting young girls … including a Russian girl at the uni who complained about him.'

At this I remember an earlier part of the evening just after the senior poet had started to read, when a voice outside the hall (obviously Donald's) had shouted something about 'fondling the buttocks of young girls' … I assumed at the time that it was just him being drunk and disorderly, as in the days when he us to write abusive letters to people (the editor of Poetry NZ most prominent among them—though Donald did (finally) apologise for that …).

⋆

The review … tried to sum up the novelist's personality in a few words:
Intelligence: average.
Character: epileptic.
Scholarship: sloppy.
Storytelling ability: chaotic.

Prosody: chaotic.

German usage: chaotic.

—Roberto Bolaño, *2666* (2004): pp. 27–28.

    ★

The cops, Myra continues, had seemed quite concerned about it—as if nowadays no such accusation can be dismissed readily as baseless, for fear of repercussions later. So it begins to look as if, rather than simply getting a bit the worse for wear and being thrown out of a venue (as happens to Craig most nights of his life, and various others depressingly often also), Donald actually came to Northcote with the intention of confronting the senior poet.

Is the story true? Obviously there's no reason to suppose so. It's not the best way to make an accusation against anyone, anyway. I feel a bit angry that he used this reading to come over and cause a stir … if that really was the motive. Perhaps it was just a story they all improvised, or embroidered a little, to get the police off their backs …

Kind of sickens you a bit with the 'literary life', though, doesn't it? The voice of a writer droning on about the imaginary dilemmas of her alcoholic character, while a real alcoholic character (which is what I'm beginning to fear Donald may be) is brawling and disintegrating under our noses.

And yet there was also something irresistibly amusing about the whole thing: the senior poet's complete and utter glee at having proved himself in combat in defence of his lady ('You missed all the excitement!' he shouted to Myra when she came sidling up); the looks on the faces of some of the Northcote ladies—poets unfettered just a bit too close for comfort; Myra picking up the gossip a mile a minute …

No one was hurt and not much got damaged (far more glasses were broken by people knocking them with their elbows), but I do feel bad for the organisers and the gallery owners. They put a lot of work into the whole thing.

Most of the poetry that was read was (predictably) dreadful, but that's not a mortal sin either.

    ★

... there was something revelatory about the taste of this bookish young pharmacist ... who clearly and inarguably preferred minor works to major ones. He chose *The Metamorphosis* over *The Trial*, he chose *Bartleby* over *Moby-Dick*, he chose *A Simple Heart* over *Bouvard and Pécuchet*, and *A Christmas Carol* over *A Tale of Two Cities* or *The Pickwick Papers*. What a sad Paradox, thought Amalfitano. Now even bookish pharmacists are afraid to take on the great, imperfect, torrential works, books that blaze paths into the unknown. They choose the perfect exercises of the great masters. Or what amounts to the same thing: they want to watch the great masters spar, but they have no interest in real combat, when the great masters struggle against that something, that something that terrifies us all, that something that cows us and spurs us on, amid blood and mortal wounds and stench.
—Roberto Bolaño, *2666* (2004), p. 227.

    ★

Tell me if you'd like to hear more of this sort of thing, or if you're relieved not to *have* to hear about the mad antics of your writerly friends ... I just thought it might amuse you, but now that I look at it I guess it's not all that amusing after all.

It's certainly a reading that will go down in North Shore history, though.

Lots of love from

Jack

D.R. JONES

Connections: A New Zealand novel in 223 words

Ake used to eel in Ohariu, where his hīnaki got so full it dragged him under.

John, from Eketahuna, sells insurance. He's trying to be a city slicker.

Lily rows her clinker on the Mahurangi Harbour, and laments the urban creep to its shores.

Jemima suffers from premature menopause—lost all the babies she never had, her friends indelicately remind her.

Garry drives a truck; takes pills to stay awake and pills to sleep.

Brendan sleeps under a bridge and turns tricks for repressed men.

Tanya flies model planes because her dad won't let her study to be a pilot like he was.

All of these people are connected.

Ake, after his near-death experience, moved to Auckland and slept rough, and goes by the name of Brendan.

Brendan gave Garry a blowjob in Galatos Street, behind K Road.

Jemima, childless, is married to John—who desperately wants kids, and is having an affair with Tanya, and plans to leave Jemima one day when he plucks up the courage (which he has never possessed). They built a bach at Mahurangi West with all the money they saved by not having to feed and clothe and educate another human.

It is Jemima's bach in particular that Lily despises, with its stainless steel railings all the way down the ostentatious boat ramp to the water's edge.

RIEMKE ENSING

Otago Harbour

From the Caselberg Trust House, Broad Bay, Dunedin, 20 February – 6 March 2015

There's no way this water could ever be 'the colour of sky'
as I read in romantic fiction recently. It's grey, dark with green
rolling in shadows even on summer days like this when it bounces with glitter
like off-loaded fish about to be scaled. Not ominous, not chilling
but with that touch of cold always recalling the dead, perished
building walls or wrecked or smashed by whales in torment.
The dead are not dead. They live with us. Every night
we set the table, leaving a space for quiet and unquiet echoes.
We give thanks.
Over years, the table gets bigger
and bigger. Soon we'll have to move out to make room.
Already memory proves deficient, to protect us.
I make lists, record birth dates and gather what photographs I can.
'Poetry is full of facts. The beating heart of history—the trapdoor
to something else' a poet tells me. He also said 'Yes' to massive wharves
blocking the harbour and its views in a city not his own.
How the land swarms with the invisible. They wear those pelts of brooding
green McCahon lashed to his hills, gold cloaks that blow in from the sea.
They're so close you can hear them breathe in the waves.

BRETT CROSS

Jacob Behmen Visits the Hauraki Plains

leading his donkey on to the dirty brown
olive-green of the plains
                    ragged napsack bouncing
off gamey flanks Jacob

set up a temple of skin over sticks
meditated and prayed
                    he wrote what troubled him
not for publication

and the visions he saw a giant curled dragon
black as the peat
                    beneath the heart of the land
in the sky a thatch of sticks bursting

to flame and a sword vast
as Maumaupaki
                    standing upright point billowing
out to engulf the plains

COURTNEY SINA MEREDITH

Land's End

The Ks are high, the Ks are low
but the seats are uncomfortable
oh spaghetti, couldn't have that:
he's Arabian on the hustle
trying to make ends meet.
I wrap a hand around, both ways,
could the dog fit—and the shine:
would they laugh me out of Run Club?

Is this really the best price in the city
the best price in New Zealand in fact?
He mutters, hosing down the silver hole,
black hole really, money guzzler.

May as well open my window,
push out the French doors, throw
everything I saved to live off
only to come to a head, land's end.

Unfair, whatever you're saving
can't be a lifelong raft, life insurance.
I made an enquiry, but I'll never know
twirling in the hot earth ... Presume
whoever I chose knows what colour
brings out my eyes

then again, they'll be closed ...

He rings an hour later says, thick accent,
and it's hurting his throat all the way:
a hundred dollars off my dear

because you know, he's made a loss
and I must've looked around of course—
made a point of searching
similar creatures, adequate plots ...

Had I not imagined
having to compromise
one day, finally?

Silence, awkward pause.
God I spent hours thinking about this moment,
there's a history on my Mac to prove it
so I can't go forgetting what I've lost.

Petrol is cheap but house prices are soaring.
You have to pay your respects to the roof
over your head, before it spins
into the sun.

CAROLYN McCURDIE

Turn

I was numb in those years,
walked down that road till she stopped me.
She had my name, my face, head sunk into her shoulders,
feet scuffing the gravel, where I came behind.

Her mind was a shrunken thing that lived six feet deep,
nothing to see but the seep and shine
of the spade-shaped clay, a future
of shovel-loads dropping on skull.

My name, my face—a tightness that said: give nothing,
trust no one, hit back whenever you can.
I never met her. She turned towards me
in time to prevent it.

Because of her I shed my skin.
With a knife I'd found under my pillow
I hacked at the tethers that pulled me to her
till the inevitable lay on the verge like roadkill.

And that road was no longer mine. A turning.
Without armour, into tree-dark beginnings and questions.
What is face?
What is name?

Summer

You must've stunk, musky, skunky hippie
walking up the road to Jerusalem.

Your bare feet pressed the dust,
like it would always be summer.

Heat shimmered over the verges,
ox-eyes shivered in an almost-breeze.

What magnet pulled you?
Love is not a recent thing.

Bees did waggle-dances,
wood beetles sang in the empty house.

★

The thousand curves in the old bus,
the walk through nauseous groves.

But I don't *want* to see
a blue duck, whines a child.

Youth stretched in the grass,
deep in Dickens.

A girl beside him,
her head strung with beads.

Like a bride who wears
her dowry in her hair.

*

All the life in London:
a wandering piglet.

Dark and lovely
a Greek woman smiles
under the road sign at Athens.

The convent's florid bedspreads.
Its table under poplars.

My skin's come off,
cries the child in his sleep,
my bones are hanging out.

*

A girl writes the marae names
in her curly script

on the song sheet.
Ehara i te mea, nō ināianei te aroha.

Hutia te rito o te harakeke
Kei whea te kōmako e kō?

As scones are served
a woman strums and sings

Someone loves you, honey
Wherever you go.

*

You used to hold your arms
out, cruciform,

your long hair hung
around your shoulders.

Beard touching your chest.
Guitar slung over your groin.

Cancer gave you
friendly muttonchops.

You say you paddled here
from Taumarunui, alone.

*

Everyone who passes
seems to know you, thin traveller.

The spine of the woman
beside you curves,
breast drooping to her child's mouth.

You talk of community,
part ways at your campervan.

It is Christmas.
Kate is waiting for you.
And Mary has a cake in the oven.

Rewa

In 2009, following a period of unemployment, Work and Income assigned me a six-month job as a Town Centre Ambassador in Manurewa. This job involved patrolling the town for six hours a day, noting incidents and encounters. The following is taken from the Ambassador's diary.

1.

Automobile backed out of alley into car headed south along Great South Road. Drivers argued, calmed them down, cleared traffic lanes, recorded details.

Stray pitbull terrier crossed Station Road into Northcrest parking lot, scavenging food. Called the dog pound.

Prostitute acting in disorderly manner near primary school. Called the Prostitutes' Collective to discuss the situation. They suggest setting up a meeting. Prostitute later apologised for her disorderly behaviour.

Received complaint about a red four-door sedan parked in alley by ASB. Observed four drunk male occupants verbally harassing shoppers. Informed them that they were drinking in an alcohol ban area and that their behaviour was offensive. They left.

Followed drinking man down Newhook Lane to Northcrest where he boarded a bus and left Manurewa.

Found abandoned burnt-out automobile in Northcrest carpark.

Nose-to-tail car accident at corner of Station and Great South Roads.

Followed man wearing a face-mask into Southmall.

Confronted five people drinking behind Tadmor Hall. Moved them on and cleared up their mess. Found three pieces of ID on the ground. Followed the group to Southmall. Handed ID to police.

2.

External sewer pipe broken on Liquor City building. Owner repaired it with gaffer tape.

Retrieved supermarket trolley from Tadmor Creek. (Got covered in mud in the process.)

Honda stationwagon turned across Great South Road and blocked traffic outside Wholesale Meats. Informed driver that her actions were dangerous and impeding traffic flow. Driver was offended.

Informed man in Station Road that he was drinking in an alcohol ban area. He surrendered his drink.

Report of man flashing a teenager in the Maich Road toilets. Observed suspicious male lingering around Northcrest carpark.

Articulated truck blew an airbrake and stopped outside St Andrew's Church on Great South Road. Checked that everything was OK.

Saw three Papakura High School girls tagging in alleyway by railway line. Followed them on foot through Old Recreation Centre grounds, south along Russell Road, and then into James Road. Approached and questioned them under a tree at the end of James Road. Security attended.

Three young women snatched bag on Great South Road. Followed them down Maich Road.

Observed students drinking alcohol around car in Gallaher Park. Followed them back to Great South Road.

3.

Chased trespassed offender from Southmall up Lupton Road.

Helped drunk guy to seat.

Lemons and potatoes stolen from pensioner's garden in Tadmor Retirement Village.

Helped old lady fix and secure gate.

Followed two teenage girls carrying alcohol. Caught them drinking on railway station platform. Informed them that they were drinking in an alcohol ban area and saw them on to train out of Rewa.

Old lady tripped and fell while getting out of taxi by Northcrest tunnel. Assisted her to doctor's offices.

4 .

Teenagers fighting out front of Southmall. Broke up fight.

Asked elderly man busking outside post office to move further down the road to front of Southmall.

Pākehā man and girlfriend arguing outside Halver Road toilets.

Security guard at ASB informed me that an elderly lady had been robbed in the alley adjoining the ASB. Police attended. Suspect identified.

Observed a gang associate helping to co-ordinate a car break-in at the Station Road carpark. Chased two males on foot through carpark. Lost them after they crossed the railway track. Saw them again later in the day in McAnnalley Street.

Tagging on wall outside Halal Meat and Spice shop on Great South Road.

Baby and little boy left unattended in car outside Westpak Bank on Great South Road.

Old man tripped and fell on kerb on Great South Road.

5.

Intervened to stop a fight between teenage girls outside Southmall. Police and mall security attended. Offending girls trespassed from mall.

Car backed into Mitsubishi truck in rail interchange carpark. Left note with details and our contact phone number for the truck owner.

Cut down and removed real estate sign on top of post office building as it was falling apart in high winds and endangering public safety.

Found shopping bag at bus stop on corner of Halver and Great South Roads. Contacted owner, who claimed it the next day.

Observed Pākehā lady drinking gin on street. Informed her that she was drinking in an alcohol ban area.

Rescued injured bird outside Mitsubishi Motors on Great South Road. Took bird to vet.

Approached nine-year-old boy sitting alone outside Joe's Bar on Great South Road. Found his father drinking inside and told him that he was doing wrong. The man took the child and left.

6.

Caught persistent offender in alleyway and beat him up. Public assisted until
offender ran away but was apprehended by police.

Front window at Golden Dragon Restaurant on Station Road smashed.

Stopped fight between students from Greenmeadows and Manurewa
Intermediate Schools.

Helped blind lady waiting for 455 bus, after bus driver would not help her.

A young woman complained about being threatened by a gang member.
Recorded details.

Observed man sniffing glue outside bar. Approached and took glue bag off
him.

Domestic argument between man and woman outside Southmall. Police
attended.

Reported broken upstairs window at corner of Maich and Station Roads.

7.

Two men and a woman fighting in ASB lobby. Intervened and waited for them
to leave the area. Some people have no concept of the difference between
public and private space.

Car abandoned in Station Road carpark. Rear window broken. Car keys on
floor. Reported to police.

Responded to call about students fighting in alley next to ASB. Police
attended and apprehended two students.

Lace Shop proprietor informed us that a group of people was drinking behind
her shop. While responding we noticed a little boy running alone down
Station Road. Collected the child. Moved drinkers on. Returned boy to
mother after she came forward.

Southmall evacuated after fire alarm.

Found bench seat at Maich Road taxi rank removed to other side of road.
Carried it back to its proper place.

8.

Māori woman threatening Indian woman in Rockyz carpark. Intervened.
Police attended.

Transgenders soliciting outside ASB.

Dog bit elderly woman outside Southmall drycleaners. Police attended. Turns out I knew the old lady. Why do so many people bring their dogs into the town centre?

Swarm of bees settled on car in alley next to ASB. Resolved by mall security.

Old lady locked keys in car by bowling club.

Another old lady lost and confused.

Fight in front of Southmall. Police attended.

Young woman collapsed in front of Southmall. Doctor and ambulance attended.

9.

Black Power gang member says he hates the colour red in our uniforms and asks if I am a recruiter for the Mongrel Mob.

10.

Domestic dispute at railway station. Man jumped in front of train. Emergency services attended. Foot left on railway track.

11.

Feeling unwell. Returned to office and lay down. (This shit is making me sick.)

12.

Assisted old lady crossing intersection at Great South and Station Roads.

Rubbish bin removed from mounting in Station Road carpark. Reported it to council. There are a lot of dumb people around here with nothing better to do than make a nuisance of themselves.

Plants destroyed outside post office.

Gave tourists information (Get out of town—nicer further north).

Gave man directions to bus stop and bus route information.

Confiscated alcohol from woman drinking in Station Road carpark.

Prostitute caused disturbance at opening of new civic square.

13.

Escorted shop owner carrying cash to bank.

Rival gang members arguing outside Joe's Bar. (More dumb shit.)

Assisted small child walking alone across Great South Road.

Found broken statue outside Sushi Bar on Station Road. This looked like
statue reported stolen in the local paper. Notified police.

We ambassadors assembled and marched in Santa Parade. Mayor attended.
(What a politician!)

Nicole Page-Smith, 'Untitled', 2008.

New Aoteasamoa

My name is Eleni. It's a name from Samoa, the birthplace of my parents. The vowels are pronounced like those of the native Māori alphabet, but te reo wasn't promoted in New Zealand back in the 1970s. Hence, my name stammered out of palagi or Pākehā mouths as Eeleeneye.

*

Wh-tch!

The sting of Miss Ellen's leather strap burned the palm of my hand. Miss Ellen was my primer two teacher at primary school.

'Eeleeneye, I'm speaking to you!' she said.

I was being punished for standing up for myself. Sarah Wilkinson had lied. She told our teacher I had ripped her crayon drawing for nothing. I had tried to reveal the truth, but Miss Ellen had already brought out the thick leather strap from the bottom drawer of her desk and, scrunching the part of my cardigan behind my neck into her fist, had pulled me to the front of the classroom.

So I shut my mouth, bowed my head, held out my hand like Miss Ellen told me to, and waited. My Samoan upbringing taught me to respect my elders and not talk back.

Wh-tch!

The pain was sharper.

'Did you hear me, Eeeleeneye? I said look at me!'

The blue carpet became a watery blur as tears overflowed from my eyes. I was confused. I wasn't supposed to look elders in the eye when they were talking, especially when being reprimanded. It was a sign of disrespect and defiance. Yet, I was also supposed to obey my elders without question.

Wh-tch!

My hand burned and started to tremble uncontrollably. My silent weeping escalated into hiccupping sobs.

'LOOK AT ME, YOU RUDE GIRL!'

Miss Ellen's angry words puffed through the fringe of my hair, feeling hot on my forehead.

Finally, I slowly raised my head.

Red blotches were spreading along Miss Ellen's cheeks and nose. It reminded me of how my blood soaked into the fabric of my dad's jersey when I tumbled off my bike and grated the skin on my legs outside Eden Park. Miss Ellen looked like a firecracker ready to explode.

'Next time,' she said, jutting her face closer to mine, 'do as you're told the first time I tell you!' Spittle from her barking snarl sprayed my already wet cheeks.

How could she terrify children by forcing them to watch her full-blown wrath and hate? If I misbehaved in front of my elders, they gave me loud, long lectures that included common Samoan sayings—empty threats such as 'I'll stomp on your head, you shit eater.' Sure, sometimes I'd feel the whack of a belt or jandal, but never had I witnessed horrifying, shape-shifting rage until Miss Ellen's strap incident.

During the following days, Miss Ellen would grip my chin in her thumb and index finger, and pull my face towards hers when speaking to me. I found it excruciatingly uncomfortable undoing the conditioning of my Samoan upbringing, but I didn't want to unleash the white dragon with the fiery face again, and so within a week I was able to make and keep eye contact without needing Miss Ellen's 'guidance'.

Then came the day I lost my prescription glasses at school. We weren't rich, not even average back then, so my dad was furious. I sat on the floor in front of him, crying as he yelled at me. I didn't realise I had started staring at him until he stopped in the middle of his rant, his eyes widening in shock.

In Samoan he said, 'How dare you look at me—and like that!'

Whack.

★

My birthplace is Aotearoa; it's reclaiming its nativeness. Now, my elders are less offended when people hold eye contact. My name, Eleni, is not so hard to pronounce any more.

ERIK KENNEDY

Georgics

A lambent light it is that fills the pasture, but it's too dark to read.
The wise farmer rises early to get the best broadband speed.

As shepherds watch their fleecy care, they see claggy-arsed,
    beady-eyed billows of wool.
A full house is a pair of Cheviots and three of a kind of Karakuls.

'Pneumatic nipple suck-fest' is a quaint term for the morning milking!
Gervase Markham writes of a cow that filled sixty buckets.

You can ride a tractor from, as the Italians say, the stable to the stars.
The tractor's GPS is more powerful than the computer on the ship that,
    some day, will take men to Mars.

Fifty miles south of here it's green-yellow. Fifty miles north it's green.
Here, brown trout are scooped from the drying river in nets and trucked
    to the sea.

They wrap hay in plastic now, another processed food.
'They' are the farmers. Making hay is a pleasant interlude.

The last lightning-strike fire was put out by passing farmer Alan Maclehose.
The superstitious among us say that he throws the lightning himself.

I've asked, and my duty is not to protect the weak.
It is to make the weak strong. May they use that strength to make
    their own peace.

Sheep's eyes at night from a car look like the ghosts of snooker balls.
The dew falls in orbs and rises in a vaporous pyramid. That's the water cycle,
    kid.

The half-sun on the evening hill is a great-aunt's hairy kiss.
Around the manger the animals sing 'What Version of Pastoral is This?'

Where the glow-worm creepeth in the night, no adder will go in the day.
The ways things are going now, it's cheaper to throw the crops out
    than to give them away.

NICHOLAS REID

The Petrified Forest at Curio Bay

There are two deadnesses here.
One is the arboreal rock
looking charred from yesterday's fire,
black bark, orangey-pink inside,
but cold and solid to the touch.
Indubitably rock.

And one is this unquestioning assent of mine.
It's only rock like any other.
I'm one of those tourists who need
the noticeboard above, designed
to point an ancient forest's petrification
in these broken seashore lines.

I try to work a passion up
and feel what I am meant to feel—
reverence, awe perhaps, at
the aeons of time, images of
stegosauri, lands rising and falling,
human smallness, stars exploding,
the giddiness of our planetary speck.

It doesn't work. The best I can do
is a page from a child's encyclopedia,
overprinted, garish, Technicolor
crude, A Prehistoric Forest,
with dragonflies the size of lizards,
volcanoes, balloon-shaped trees.

The wind is cold. There's nothing
but grey sea between here and
the Pole. Rock is rock. Awe
cannot be faked. Real memory goes
no further back than a
childhood encyclopedia.

Before the childhood book
there is no memory.

LEONARD LAMBERT

A Window on the Inward Isles

The European Masters *exhibition at* Te Papa Tongarewa

After the Monets, Redon Rousseau Cézanne
(and, be it said, some lumber-room art, shockingly bad),
the New Zealand section is suddenly a dull encounter
in a dim province. How can this be?
The paintings seem to turn away
as if they'd adopted the Māori gaze, the non-challenge
of the averted eye. Go away, they seem to say. Leave us alone.
Do you think we're here
to make a spectacle of ourselves like those Frenchies?
Local in the worst sense, genteel, the great McCahon,
even mad Clairmont, and my beloved Brent Wong
an empty gesture. Grahame Sydney's best,
the cleverly angled one of his wife, merely domestic,
biographic, anything koru-based simply crass,
and Hotere, the most buried of all, a mere crack of light.
Who was there to say Hello? Only Frances Hodgkins,
expat. The inward islanders—is that us? Still?
It seemed so, it said so, Bugger off bugger off, every wall.

TONY O'BRIEN

White

The first white is cold, like snow,
The second colder, like ice.
The third is warm, like milk,
The fourth warmer, like skin.
The fifth white is foreboding, like a blank page.
The sixth is forgiving, like a muslin curtain drawn across a window
admitting no secrets.
There's white you can eat, like bread,
And white to drink, like coconut nectar.
There's white that floats, like cloud,
And white that sinks like stone and shines at the bottom of a pool.
Your eyes are white, your fingernails too.
There's white inside you,
White muscle sheaths, white gristle and bone.
The sharp white of your teeth cuts my flesh.
Not an innocent white, but white lust,
And in the deep of a white sleep there's no sobbing,
Just the white noise of night.

KIERAN DOODY

Imagined Madness

She is florid madness blooming vermilion red.
She is the fingernails that have bled carving the writing on the wall of the
solid asylum.
She is the primal scream that breaks the squalid silence.
She is the one clawing at the walls to make windows in the white room for
she wishes to see the beautiful moon for she know that if it turns black it will
attract more blackness.
Trapped in the darkness of the mind attic, strapped up in a chemical
strait-jacket, she is mournful and melodramatic dancing to deaf symphonies
in sincere misery.
She is part of the linoleum chessboard floor, disenchanted
by all the four corners that seem to box her in. She is taken
down the corridor for her cure, the pure bright white
lighting, blinding, binding her to an insanity she never had
but forever owns.
Her eyes opened to the divine mess.
She is left counting suicides instead of blessings, wrestling
with an angel at a table laid with sacrificial silver all the
filthier for the cleanliness of the blood that is shed.
She is emptiness and emptiness is her.
She is the dead one that still speaks to me in secrecy
through cracks in the wall.
She is sweet apocalypse, the setting sun.
I feel the end coming, it's getting closer and closer.
It's almost over as heaven falls heavy as hell.
The rains fill the flooding skin, the bloody end is just where she begins.

ANDREW M. BELL

In the Black

The market urged him to save time,
to save labour
and he was an obedient man.

The labour he saved
hung on him like festooning grapes,
plump, ripe and bursting like
his overtaxed arteries.

His labour-saving devices
saved so much time
that he ended up deep
into the black.

For Chrissie Weeping for the Sea

You're the one,
the nexus, the crux, the one at the centre
keeping all us flakes from
flaking off into a life more ordinary
and yet,
here you are, bursting into spontaneous tears,
the creep-up-behind-you emotions,
the lump rising mid-word
and it's not much to ask:
here, the poor people have a patch of the sea
not generally a city feature.

We walk our dogs, we surf our dreams and we contemplate.
We know the value of a dollar and the value of
turning your back on one.

And we're a funny, fucked-up family
and our sea is our friend,
our plaything,
our solace and we'll drive
one and a half hours
on special occasions
just to change our view of our sea
but we'll always come back to our strip
of our sea
and we'll stand and weep with our friend, Chrissie,
for the day they filled our sea with shit.

Garden of Eden Park

My father discovered social networking when he was 87. His quivering fingers didn't navigate the keyboard as smoothly as his grandchildren's did, but he persevered. He mastered email, though he preferred to write letters with his tortoiseshell fountain pen. Ashokan lion stamps glared from powder-blue envelopes in the cardboard box where I collected his correspondence.

I gave Dad a laptop when I visited him in India three years ago. I hoped he'd connect with family all over the world. It was to save him from loneliness.

'Look at my machine,' he told friends. 'It's from my son in New Zilland.' I taught him to email and introduced him to social media.

A flurry of internet activity ensued on my return. I sent photos of my wife and children, uploaded the kids' artwork. I made friend suggestions for relatives in Europe and America. My nephew posed in cricket whites on his grandfather's timeline. Dad chatted with aunts in America and nieces in Norway. He loved simultaneously exchanging information between Wisconsin, Oslo and Auckland.

There were jokes, links to songs and images of my mother smiling through dense foliage. Monsoon-charged air wrapped me in its wet warmth as I remembered Mum's embrace, the velvet of her cheek. I imagined she was still alive.

My brother posted a picture of Dad at the cricket at Eden Gardens in Kolkata. It was an old photo with a tea stain on the corner. Underneath, a string of comments grew. I suggested Dad return to Auckland. The cricket may not be as good at Eden Park, but it would be nostalgic for him. However, the frailty of old age was marking my father's bones, making travel difficult.

Dad's fingers, deformed by arthritis, found it difficult to punch computer keys. Late last year he lost patience with his 'machine', and that was the end of his cyber-experience. His accounts remain active, and people post messages on birthdays and festivals. He never reads them.

★

I get a warm feeling when I recall how serendipity knocked on my office door last month. My supervisor only just caught me as I left one evening.

Can you spare a minute?

He pulled a folder out of a drawer.

Robin can't make the Indian meeting. Can you go?

Dad was sick. I didn't have enough leave to visit him.

I'll go, I said without hesitation.

At my desk I clicked under the koru logo:

Air New Zealand

Asia … Rest of world

from: Auckland

to: Kolkata

via Hong Kong

*

I flick through the in-flight magazine as we taxi along the runway. Stroking my finger over the familiar koru I find I'm too emotional to read.

It's too late.

My father died two days ago.

After the meeting, my brother and I will pour Dad's ashes into the Ganges. Two Bengali brothers side by side, with sandalwood tikkas on our foreheads.

At 33,000 feet I contemplate my father's experiences as a young man in the 1950s. He left India, set sail for a new life. Sailed on a sea of hope towards his home for the next 27 years. My brother and I were born here. It was home until the family scattered again like glass beads. My parents had missed their homeland.

I imagine father disembarking. He carries a leather case covered in stickers from previous ports of call. He locates a post office, sends a telegram home.

I visualise him finding his way. He shivers after the cocooning warmth of India. Does the fatty tang of fish and chips turn his stomach? Or is he too hungry to care? Traffic lights, Lemon and Paeroa. Are these experiences comforting or alien?

Dad reaches Auckland and his flatmate lends him his spare coat. It has holes at the elbows. Two Bengali brothers looking out for each other. My father works in a restaurant to finance his studies. The cost of phone calls to India is prohibitive. His parents don't own a telephone anyway. I visualise the blue paper, thin as a dragonfly's wing, on which he forms the words for his letters. His mother writes every week, though her feelings lose their intensity as the lines of Bengali script travel across the world.

Dad chats to Abdul-Aziz, the Pakistani waiter. Abdul-Aziz has a wife and child back home. He has another wife, a Kiwi woman whom he refers to as 'Bhhalarri'. Valerie keeps Abdul-Aziz warm on icy nights. She saves him from loneliness.

As we come in to land, vibrant squares of farmland fluoresce in yellow light. My brother will arrive soon. I check my phone while I wait. There are messages flooding onto my father's timeline. He gets messages on birthdays and festivals.

Rest in peace.

Remembering a wonderful uncle.

Always in our minds.

He'll never read them.

MERE TAITO

No Frills

the mākutu potato sack
can fly you to Raiwaqa

cocoon you in a forcefield
so you can breathe through the clouds

lower you gently outside a bedroom window

you can step off
rattle the louvre blades
wake a family

breakfast with a favourite cousin
hear her say:
grace first please

say grace
wolf the long loaf slices thickly spread with Rewa butter
guzzle the sweet milky lemon leaf tea

tell her in between mouthfuls
how much she is missed

the mākutu potato sack
will fly you back to Hamilton

cocoon you in a forcefield
so you can breathe through the rain

lower itself gently outside the kitchen window

you can step on
shut the louvre blades
wave goodbye to a family

after you have asked:
thank you for the food, may I leave the table please?

YIYAN WANG

Englishness

to be English,
    in my perspective of
someone from a provincial Chinese city
    is to be embarrassed
about everything
    remotely personal.

to avoid embarrassment
    they travel long distances
circling around and around
    the topic in mind
before they locate
    some ambiguous expressions
    to hint at
their intended meanings.

It took me years to decipher
    'would you like to have a coffee sometime?'
    is an expression of interest to
    have a conversation.

and,
    'shall we go to see a film?'
    is the preamble of
    being asked on a date.

they take care to leave plenty of space
    in case of rejection
    they are able to withdraw
    without being embarrassed.

for a non-native-English speaker
    and a total introvert
    despite the unlikeliness of such a combination
    the subtlety is permanently lost

so is the paradise of
    living happily ever after.

EMMA SHI

and never talk about forever

we can listen to the radio at midnight and kiss with glass lips
i'll pick up the phone for you at 4 am when you're asleep
tell them you're doing fine
we can catch a plane back home and look out the window and cry
slow dance to airport traffic
i'll call you my best friend i promise

JOANNA PRESTON

Hysteria

says the magazine he looks up from,
claims one passenger on average every
couple of hundred flights. My fears
are stowed in the overhead locker,
clenched in zippered teeth.
Jet fuel is twenty per cent lighter than water,
and burns at eight hundred degrees,
the magazine man tells me, and laughs,
smelling of barbecue sauce.
There's a stain the shape of Africa on his tie,
which tells me that no woman loves him.
Long-distance commercial passenger flights
typically cruise at nine hundred k's,
three-quarters the speed of a bullet.
Victorian ladies pursed pins in their lips
when travelling through railway tunnels
to guard against strangers trying to
kiss them in the dark.
The grass beside the runway is sparse
and straggly, like his hair.
Taxiing now. It feels like late summer
afternoons in the old ute,
bumping along the river flat
with a bale of hay in the back.
He's speaking again, but I keep
my eyes on the road ahead.

MURRAY EDMOND

Jack Body and Multi-Media Performance 1968-1975

I want to discuss an aspect of Jack Body's work that seemed important in the years from 1968 (after Jack had finished his MA in Music) to 1975 (when his engagement with Asian, particularly Indonesian, music begins in earnest).

In the late sixties the term 'multi-media' indicated performance work that was a mixture (sound and music, plus light, plus projected images moving and still, plus performing bodies both dancing and speaking, plus writing). This mixture aimed to decentralise the playing space and the audience's watching/listening focus. It is a delicate thing to say that coherence was not always the aim, but that actually needs to be said more definitely and even defiantly, *that coherence might be actively opposed*. Another way of saying this is that what coherence was achieved might be only discovered in performance, and on that occasion alone. It seems different, looking back, from the comprehensive use of different media in music or dance or theatre performance now, as if the heritage from that time has flowed through but taken a tributary away from the original course. In a way, the early Modernist ideal of *Gesamtkunstwerk* has been re-installed, perhaps with 'festival culture' making this more imperative.

In 1973 Jack wrote:

IN GENERAL

I WOULD LIKE MY LESSONS

TO BE IN THEMSELVES

COMPLETE

LEADING NOWHERE

IN PARTICULAR

The 'particularity of nowhere' was what was sought. Jack was describing his experiences as a music teacher at Tawa College in Wellington in an article titled 'Diary of a school music teacher' published in *Islands*. The capital letters, and the poetics and theory they proclaim, were shared by some poets, dancers and theatre-makers as well as other composers. There was a kind of work being looked for. Everyone looking for it might do other kinds of things from time to time, as Jack did, but this 'multi-media event' loomed large as a possibility in its very own particularity of nowhere.

There was also a division for him between music in its sophisticated High Modernist manifestation and music in its populist ephemeralness. I remember well the uncomprehending mix of horror and bewilderment on Jack's face when we literary types played our Arlo Guthrie and Led Zeppelin records. But he was also drawn to the populist part of the spectrum. The wonderful poster for his *Sexus* featured an androgynous young man with bare torso who could have been Mick Jagger by way of The Pretty Things. *Sexus* was quite a tough show—film footage shot by Jack showed the spilling guts of the slaughtered beasts in an abbatoir—yet it was also a kind of dark circus about sexuality, repression, and Kiwiland, as only someone from Te Aroha (the town's name is its irony) could know. Jack had a sense of what things each were in their integrity—and also how these things might be mixed up. The mixture always intrigued him, and getting the balance, the mix, right was the source of excitement and frustration.

Young Aucklanders in the Arts 1968

Young Aucklanders in the Arts was a festival presented over three nights in the cafeteria of the recently completed Student Union building at Auckland University. The festival was presented by the Auckland Society for Contemporary Music which had, until then, been involved in staging concerts of determinedly Modernist music (Boulez, Stockhausen, Lou Harrison); however, these concerts had been 'quite formal, with small audiences' and held at the City Art Gallery. The festival featured work by Body and by composers Robin Maconie and Noel Sanders. But it was not a music festival. Poets Alan Brunton, Sam Hunt, Alan Trussell-Cullen, Michael Jackson and Ian Wedde read their poetry; Francis Batten presented mime à la Marcel Marceau; Russell Haley's play *The Running European* was staged (with Stephen Gordon later of the Living Theatre Troupe playing the role of Sheperd), and there were exhibitions of paintings.

I was 18 years old, in my first year at university; my English tutor was Juliet Batten. Juliet's husband was Francis Batten and her brother was Michael Jackson. It must have been through this connection that I came to participate in the piece that Jack presented. I had gone to university to study Japanese (which I had already been learning for a year at school) and Chinese, and I was enrolled for two courses of first-year Chinese and two courses of first-year Japanese. Juliet would have known this and she must have suggested that I go along to the rehearsal of Jack's piece, because he was looking for people who could make sounds in different languages.

So, while Jack stood centre stage a number of us formed a semi-circle with access to a few microphones and, when Jack pointed at us, we stepped up to the microphone and made our language sounds. Perhaps there wasn't even a score and Jack really improvised the whole thing on the spot. I do not remember. Mostly my execrable Mandarin tones mesmerised me into a state of embarrassment. But the whole festival proved to be a marvellous feast: an event unique in its innovation, its loose and open format. I went to everything and listened and looked, soaking it all up. Thank you, Jack.

Turtle Time

Russell Haley's poem 'Turtle Time' was published in the *New Zealand Universities' Arts Festival Yearbook 1969*. Before 'Turtle Time' received this literary publication, it had become the words for a musical setting by Jack Body in 1968. *Turtle Time*, the composition, had its premiere at one of the Contemporary Music Society concerts. Haley's poem consists of two pages of wild verbal gambits about time:

> There are so many incredible doors
> on which I must still pin notes
> for people who arrived
> yesterday
> they listen
> and they laugh at me tomorrow
> I have committed
> a ritual death of clocks

Haley's interior traumas and phantasms grow legs and run all over the page and the streets:

> When you walk through the spittled streets
> with money sewn in the lining

of your pinstriped coat
you know it's only a question of time
before you attach your testament
of solitude
on doors and
faces.

But the poem is not all from the poet's mindscape. Arthur Stace (1885–1967), who is estimated to have written the word 'eternity' in chalk with copperplate letters on the streets of Sydney half a million times between 1932 and 1967, enters the poem, his insistent scorings being something that Haley had seen while living in Sydney:

I have wandered the streets
of Wooloomooloo
at night
writing ETERNITY
on pavements with
yellow chalk
and gone to bed with the sour
taste of a brass clock
ticking under my tongue.

Body set the poem to a score for piano, organ, harp, harpsichord and speaking voice; and the energy and exuberance of the music matches the language.

The Stations of the Cross and *The Resurrection*

At Easter 1969, Jack Body combined sound he had assembled at Douglas Lilburn's Electronic Music Studio at Victoria University with a text by poet Ian Wedde, and contributions from kinetic sculptor Leon Narbey, lighting designer Keir Volkerling and painter David Armitage. *The Stations of the Cross*, staged in the Maclaurin Chapel at Auckland University, was pitched in the *Auckland Star* as 'a contemporary theatre presentation experience'.

Jack may have wondered if religion lacked the grace to leave him alone when I turned up, a little later that year, at 27 Birdwood Crescent to ask if he would compose music for the songs that open and close W.B. Yeats' play *The Resurrection* (1931), in which a Hebrew, a Greek and a Syrian argue about the nature of the Messiah, and Christ himself makes a surprise appearance, 'wearing a recognisable but stylistic mask', towards the end of the play. The play does not represent Yeats at his most dynamic and the combination of my virginal directing abilities with a young student cast from the drama society of the university, then known as the Five and Nine Club, meant the production bogged down in words beyond measure, or so it felt to me when it was performed in June 1969. The play opens with a poem and closes with a poem, known as 'Two Songs from a Play'. They were published in Yeats' 1928 volume *The Tower* and they are the best things in the play. As well as the actors, Yeats gives the play 'three Musicians', and throughout the text regularly requests that 'the Musicians make faint drum-taps, or sound a rattle'. Ngahuia Volkerling, now Ngahuia Te Awekotuku, sang the songs and the musicians played Jack's score, of which it is the percussion that has stayed in my mind.

Sexus and Nu Zac

Jack Body was overseas, mainly in Germany, from the second half of 1969 through to late 1971, returning home through Asia. His first few months back were spent in the family bach at Waihi Beach. During 1972 he shared a flat with several of us, including myself, at 24 Morgan Street, an old wooden cottage near the Domain in Newmarket, which had been home to Jean and Russell Haley and their children Ian and Cathy before they went overseas. Jack was working as a secondary school teacher, paying off his studentship loan, struggling to endure the daily torments of the classroom. He was also working on *Sexus*. *Sexus* was ambitious in scale, a music/dance/film piece that was staged in concert (sic) with a performance of Stockhausen's 1968 work *Kurzwellen* at the Maori Community Centre near Victoria Park. *Sexus* was part of the New Zealand Universities' Arts Festival held in Auckland in August 1972, and it shared the festival programme with events such as Wystan Curnow's word and image presentation *The Bombing of Auckland*, Theatre Action and the Living Theatre Troupe's anti-war *Masked March* down Queen Street, and Phil Dadson's staging of Cornelius Cardew's *The Great Learning*.

The subject of *Sexus* was sex: 'Without the lustiness of sex, religion is joyless and abstract; without the self-abandonment of religion, sex is mechanical masturbation.' Religion even wormed its way in here as this quotation from American Zen-oriented Alan Watts adorned the front of the programme. Among the six dancers were Warwick Blanchett, Deborah Hunt and Jennifer Shennan, with Jennifer as choreographer. Deborah and Jennifer would go on to join Theatre Action for their show *Adventures* in October 1972, and Warwick would join that company in 1973. Despite the rather Blakean passion of the Watts quotation, there was a coolness and a darkness to *Sexus*: pale, body-stocking-clad dancers (the naked dancer had yet to appear on the arthouse stage) moved under, around and over one another on the rather distant stage of the Maori Community Centre. The centre, along with Ngati Poneke, one of the proto-urban marae, was ill-lit, a dark, cavernous and shadowy space, and a certain indistinctness remains my lasting memory; this and the guts of the sheep spilling into the offal tray as the film from the killing chain of a freezing works near Te Aroha flickered on the screen.

Sexus was essentially a work of theatre, though the Stockhausen remained a music-qua-music performance. For me music was another country. One day I told Jack I was tone deaf. 'No one is tone deaf,' he replied. And he took me to his room where he had a clavichord he used for composing. (His room was quite small, and to give himself more space he had built his bed on top of a wardrobe, and the clavichord was housed in the alcove under the bed.) He played some notes: 'Sound that one, and that one and that one ... well, maybe some people are tone deaf!' Then he offered me a solution. Anything you hear—the closing of a door, the purring of a cat, the passing of a car—try to imitate it. He was suggesting that I start *listening*.

In October 1972 Theatre Action mounted a show called *Adventures* at Central Theatre in Remuera. The 'adventures' were in the combination of music and movement. As Francis Batten, director of Theatre Action, explained, 'It was a series of explorations into the realm of movement and contemporary music.' Composers whose music was used in the show included Edgar Varèse, Rainer Riehn, Gyorgy Ligeti, Pharaoh Sanders and Warwick Blanchett, who had danced in *Sexus*. Jennifer Shennan tells us that the Varèse and the Ligeti were Jack's suggestions. Batten went on to say, 'In our approach we had tried to enter and come to terms with the music.' The work was neither quite dance, nor quite theatre: 'The imagery of our epoch is different and we have to find it.'

The final piece in the show, which took up the whole second half, was a new soundscape by Jack Body, titled Nu Zac. The majority of members of Theatre Action were French or Canadian graduates from L'Ecole Jacques Lecoq in Paris. Nu Zac was partly their attempt to make a statement about New Zealand society after nearly a year living and working here. One of the main images in Nu Zac was the pedestrian-crossing buzzer on a pole. When this buzzer was activated, the whole company set off on the Barnes dance of a pedestrian crossing, interweaving, while carefully avoiding any contact with one another. The deeply ingrained Kiwi practice of avoiding intimacy was captured in this sound and movement image.

The Serenity Festival 1972

The Serenity Festival was held in Whanganui at the end of 1972. It was a one-off festival that seemed to be connected to James K. Baxter's death shortly before. Blerta gave a concert in the field below Four Seasons Theatre, and Theatre Action performed a masked comedy in the same field. Up in the Four Seasons, Beggar's Bag Theatre (Paul Carew, Mary Paul, Sally Rodwell and myself) performed Games We Play in protest at the proposed Springbok rugby team's tour in 1973. Jack was also there. At dusk he handed anyone who wanted a whistle and a balloon with the instructions: 'Blow your whistle and let go your balloon.' It could have been over in five seconds, but instead the magical simplicity of the instructions meant that the 'piece' went on into the day's end. The instructions were so open and so inviting that the participants immediately began to build the score/script/text/instruction/provocation. They climbed the steep hill behind Four Seasons Theatre building. They emerged onto a plateau of farmland with paddocks of cows. They spread out, blowing their whistles and randomly releasing their balloons, while in response the cows began to shift and move in what looked like patterns. For one watching, as I was, the whole thing seemed to be endowed with structure and intent. Perhaps the cows knew.

New Dance '73 and Sound Movement Theatre 1975

In 1973 Jack Body was given six weeks' leave from his teaching job at Tawa College to tour with New Dance '73. It was the first national tour by a modern dance group. It was logical that Jack should be at this beginning, since, in a way, with his involvement with dance, movement, sound and music, he had already begun. The 1975 national tour by the ad hoc company Sound Movement Theatre—dancers John Casserley and Char Hummel, composers Jack Body and Barry Margan, poet Bill Manhire, painter Ralph Hotere—was described by Cathy Wylie as 'theatre's most significant 1975 production'. The programme was in two halves; first half, *Song Cycle* (involving all the artists named above), and second half, *Anatomy of a Dance*, solely Jack Body's work, danced by Indonesian dancer Kuat Suhadji. Wylie commented, 'Jack Body's *Anatomy of a Dance* could not have succeeded unless it had been multi-media … but here the multi-media form came from one artist only.' *Anatomy* used three elements: 'a dulled American voice reciting the side effects of physical training', Kuat Suhadji's dancing, and three screens for projecting still photographs of the dancer and his dance. Wylie wrote in her review: 'It is novel, and possibly a little disconcerting for audiences, who … are accustomed to theatre performances of one focus only.'

The Second Sonic Circus: *Sonic 2*, 1975

The idea for the *Sonic Circuses* was imported, but under Jack Body's compositional organisation they can be seen as the culmination of the theatrical and multi-media approach to performance that Jack had been developing since 1968. The first *Sonic Circus* in 1974 had presented the work of 17 New Zealand composers over six hours in the Victoria University Student Union. The second *Sonic Circus* in March 1975 brought together 33 new New Zealand compositions in the space of four hours in the general vicinity of the Wellington Town Hall: in the main auditorium, in the Concert Chamber, in the Green Room, in the corridors, on the stairs, in the kitchen, in the foyer, in the fire escape stairwell, under the stage, in the Public Library, on the library lawn, in the sunken garden and so on. 'Compositions' were not only by composers: Theatre Action and the recently formed Red Mole also performed. There was a serious intent to be less serious behind the whole enterprise: 'Now some serious musicians have decided to make "serious" music a little less serious, less esoteric, more approachable, more "available".' Not everyone was happy with this intention, notably the professional musicians of the New Zealand Symphony Orchestra, who had been made available for the occasion. Allan Thomas noted that Noel

Sanders' 'Sacred to the Memory of Death' and Jack's 'Resonance Music' both suffered from 'grudging and dour performances by the players of the New Zealand Symphony Orchestra'.

Things came to a head over Phil Dadson's composition *On a Theme*: 'the opportunity seemed a perfect one to get the orchestra to meet the audience' (Dadson). The initial instructions on the score read: 'Singly and in groups orchestra and chorus traverse the stage to and from all directions, greeting the audience and each other with warm exuberance.' The score further suggested that in place of conventional greetings, words such as 'Economy' or 'Unemployment' or 'Woolworths' or 'Depression' should be used. The conductor was given the stage instructions of entering to clapping and cheering draped in the national flag. The orchestra refused to perform. So the piece was taken away from the professionals and given to the audience. *On a Theme* became the climax of *Sonic* 2, as Cathy Wylie attested: 'There was a surprise treat at the end … it consisted of Philip Dadson leading the Scratch Orchestra into a spiralling, hip-twisting, head-tossing or simply finger-tapping celebration that threatened to reach its peak and stop at any moment, but which finally wound up and up miraculously for a glorious half hour.'

Afterlife: *Runes* 1984

In 1984 Jack contributed a performance 'event' to the New Zealand Ballet Company's *New Moves* programme, featuring a series of new works by local choreographers. *Runes* was originally commissioned by Auckland City Art Gallery and it brought his photography into the performance arena. The first *Sonic Circus* had featured an erotic room, an installation by Rotorua artist Ted Bulmer, which spectators had to crawl into and lie down inside while tapes of Anna Lockwood's 'Love Field' and Jack's 'Orgasm' were played. This may have provided a model for *Runes*. In 1981 Body stated in the magazine *Canzona*:

> It is rather to the nature of the animal himself, the New Zealander, than to the landscape that we must look for the key to the characteristics of New Zealand music … What then are the stereotypical characteristics of that typical New Zealander? He belongs to a 'passionless society' where people are reticent, where sensuality is suspect, where men do not cry … Much of New Zealand music is characterised by an emotional restraint that borders on inhibition.

At first *Runes* too had been an installation. As a composition it had a double life. The photos, which were projected slides in the live performance, in the gallery were pinned to the walls of a cave-like room one entered with a torch and onto which one shone the beam of one's light, while hearing the soundtrack of water sounds recorded in toilets. *Runes* determined to show the inside of this passionless, loveless society in all its longing and desire and repression. The live piece used three screens, four slide projectors and hundreds of slides. The projected images were the runes, beginning with crude sexual drawings from the walls of public toilets. The images then moved to single words (as children begin language), utterances declaring desire, fantasies, abusive sexist statements and racist hatreds. The sequencing progressed further to whole sentences, some arranging assignations and some, especially those from women's toilets, elaborating sexual problems accompanied by pieces of advice. The piece was 20 minutes long and was accompanied by the continuous stereo soundtrack of water, which grew more and more intense. No dancers appeared on stage. Instead, it was the slide images that danced across the screens.

The Ballet Company's performance of *Runes* took place in the Memorial Theatre of Victoria University. There was a capacity audience, a large part of it made up of young Wellington ballet students. The reception was intense. As the slides clicked through, some people began to boo and hiss, while others began shouting, 'Bravo!' Jack, sitting in the audience, had not prepared himself for these reactions. But he felt the piece justified itself when he overhead a conversation between a husband and wife during the show: 'Come on, let's leave!' And the reply: 'Let's not.'

Jack could turn the bitter or cramped expression of human feeling to something open and full of life. When we flatted at 24 Morgan Street, the phone had rung one night and the call was for Jack. He put the phone down in real distress. A voice had said that it had got the phone number from the wall of the Durham Street toilet and the writing beside the number said, 'Jack Body will do anything.' We drove down with Jack to Durham Street, found it was true and erased the graffiti. The whole business was disturbing, unpleasant. But I wonder whether that moment was later turned around and used to create the world of *Runes*, with its cries of desire that move through to voices of support and advice.

Suburb

Caversham is more than I can hear
at any one time.

More than the slow drum-roll
of a goods train passing through.

More than the monotone
of a single plane in a marble sky,

the clatter of the rescue helicopter
directly overhead, the background

oceanic surge
of biddable motorway traffic.

In Caversham, I have yearned
to be closer to the horizon,

that splinter of grey
ocean you can barely see.

In Caversham I have seen wooden porches
used as podiums for beer drinkers.

Lawns covered in polystyrene hail.
A blaze of light at the end of a passage

opened to the daylight, both ends.
Caversham is the factory worker

carrying his takeaway coffee as carefully
as he would a newborn.

It's the skate-boarder towing a staffie.
The Four Square supermarket

under its careworn verandah.
The woman on her way to the Sports Dairy

in bare feet and a black t-shirt
that says, 'I Am So L.A.'

in hot-pink. It is the foxie
tied to a railing outside the Book Bus.

EMILY KARAKA

SETTLEMENT

Settlement, an exhibition of 15 large paintings, was first shown at the Orexart Gallery in Auckland during July–August 2015.

1. *Post Settlement Governance Entities*, 2015, 1000 x 1000 mm. Oil on kauri board.
2. *Matukutururu*, 2015, 1000 x 1000 mm. Oil on kauri board.
3. *Maungawhau and Maungakiekie*, 2015, 1000 x 1000 mm. Oil on kauri board.
4. *Maungarei*, 2015, 1000 x 1000 mm. Oil on kauri board.
5. *Ohuiarangi*, 2015, 1000 x 1000 mm. Oil on kauri board.
6. *Motuihe and Tiritiri Matangi*, 2015, 1000 x 1000 mm. Oil on kauri board.
7. *Rangitoto*, 2015, 1000 x 1000 mm. Oil on kauri board.
8. *Mahurangi: Maungaika and Takarunga Purchases*, 2015, 1000 x 1000 mm. Oil on kauri board.

Emily Karaka's work, Settlement, uses conventional expressionist oil painting as polemic, using vivid colour and a great deal of text to express history, elegy and anger all linked to specific areas around Auckland, particularly [its] historical volcanic cones.
— T.J. McNamara, New Zealand Herald, 1 August 2015

My work has been centred on the Treaty of Waitangi as the founding document, as the base of legislation and government in this country … It's to do with rangatiratanga, our atua, our taonga, land rights, living rights, arts and cultural rights guaranteed in that foundation document.
—Emily Karaka, quoted in *Five Māori Painters*, ed. Ngahiraka Mason
(Auckland Art Gallery Toi o Tāmaki, 2014)

TE WAI O HUA
KAI WAKA
SUB MISSION III
+ MINUTE BOOK
WAITANGI
30
330
2477
2 Horses
LARGE Boat
BLANKETS
10 FROCK COATS
100 SHIRTS
40 SHAWLS
2 PAILS
3 tents
4 SAWS
6 Bags of FLOUR
2 SADDLES
3 Bridles
MAUNGAREI
MT WELLINGTON
TURTON DEED
KOHIMARAMA
acres
AK
2101

TA MA KI

NGAITAI deed 233

ADENDUM to the 75000 ACERS

DEED...⅓ to

Return to MAORI

when HORI TE WHETUKI FLEW A white FLAG GOVENER GREY GAVE him A FLAG TO FLY GREY SAID HE WOULD NOT LOOSE HIS LAND.

when THE SON'S Ray came up the PATUPAIAREHE
TURNED to STONE

FAIR BURN BLOCK

AKITAI deed 219

TAMATERA deed 221

OHUIARANGI PIGEON MOUNTAIN

DISPUTED LAND IN AUCKLAND

E. KARAKA '15

NGA TUATARA O TAIKEHU
15 BLANKETS £5 10 SPADES
1 Pair of Trousers
1 Shirt 1 Pair of Boots 1 Vest
1 Bridle
TE WEITI
RANGITOTO
NGA PONA TORU A PERETU
TURTON DEED 232 1854
KARAKA '15

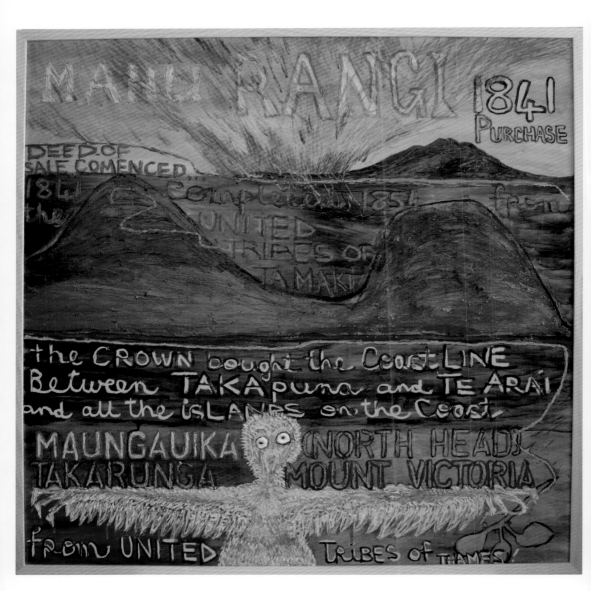

186 Leith Street

They weren't fussy about flatmates, they needed the money.
Bed squeezed in the corner, my head listening to the walls
at night, secrets tapped in mice code, in the creak of bearers
holding the room's weight at bay.

Walls wrinkled in layers of papers fraying in yellowed threads,
holding in place their scrim skin. One open-eyed night I picked
a wound that deep. Skirting the floor, dark panels were thin defence
between out and in.

Wind poked through the window's gap. Rain trespassed,
soaking the sill in a swell of splinters. Around the pane
mildew thrived in damp chill but I needed the room, couldn't
afford to be fussy.

During her single visit my mother's face grew pale and grim.
For god's sake, you're sleeping in my grandmother's room.
Her mother's room was across the hall and for once my mother
had no room to turn.

HANNAH METTNER

Reasons Ross should be happy

Tonight I'll be your barman, Ross says. He pulls vials from the pockets of his blue velvet blazer, Kraken? he proffers, Grey Goose? The jacket is like a tardis, bigger on the inside, and we work our way from the vodka, via absinthe and whisky and brandy, to the dark rum: drinking by colours. Inside the jacket he looks like Matt Smith, his British charm expanding with each drink, the tying of his floral tie into a bow because bow ties are cool. He misses most of the performance because he is sitting outside with the pigeons, writing love letters to strangers. He slips them into the letterbox like he is placing well-made bets, and fetches another drink. From his pocket he produces a list I began writing him months ago: 'Reasons Ross should be happy'. It has nothing on it! he says, flattening it across his leg. Ross is optimistic enough to believe that this is only because I forget to write them down, the reasons. That's one there: 'Ross is optimistic enough …' We add more things to the list and it becomes a poem, and so, too, do the love letters that are delivered to people who don't believe in them. The night goes on and on, and, like the tardis, like the blue blazer, it is bigger on the inside. And galactic blue.

OLIVIA MACASSEY

At Night the Incubus

Ever writhed in bed, wet with the sweat
of your desire for
        good cotton sheets?

At night the incubus comes: he comes
to take me shopping. We go into those
places with the insane expensive
            shoes, we peruse
imported hand-made pasta and matching underwear sets
or golf equipment and robot vacuums. In
the all-night malls, the incubus enthrals me
with big-screen TVs and faux fur throws,
and in the dark closed shops
            shines a torch over watches
and diamond drops and wooden dolls.

We are no strangers to duty free, the incubus and me.
We go in for fancy cars and luxurious carpets
and exotic pets and quixotic gadgets.

            The incubus knows
that I could like the taste of wine, the feel
of linen and silk;
he also knows what a sucker I am
for microfibre, and the latest books.

The incubus regales me with camel coats and the best
of winter boots, for he has surveyed my domain
and shows me what I want. Alas, I am

155

in sleep shopping,
 and waking no such thing! No matter.

By day I buy my staple rice
and tins of beans in my threadbare clothes
and try not to swear at traffic lights or
press my nose on the glass of homes as I
limp back to my humble lair, and my
mattress where, when I rest,
I soon feel right.

I have to admit, I'm more tired each time,
but I eagerly close my eyes!
For at night he will come.
At night the incubus
comes. He comes
to take
me
    shopping.

LIZ BRESLIN

Migraines for Beginners

you will need
a halo of silver foil survival just outside your eyeline
to hear the word impending thunder bright
a cheekload of nausea at the thought of your regular
several little pink spots of rage
a hard-faced ball-peen hammer
a shrinkable clamp
a metronome on slow repeat
one cold patch of pillow
time

LYNLEY EDMEADES

Some Bodies Make Babies

Not alone, of course
but with the help of a David or a James
and a house on a street in a town
with some food in the cupboards
and a grandmother to look after
the baby's big sister
when things start to happen
in a hospital with a bath
and a phone to tell all the people
who might or might not know
the meaning of contraction or dilation
of how it feels to want to get up
and walk away from yourself.

One plus one equals two
or three or four
sometimes more.
For some one plus one
equals one big empty house
with spare rooms that no one asks about
and too much leftover ham at Christmas.

Some bodies make babies
and some make none.

The Landfall Review

Landfall Review Online

www.landfallreview.com

Reviews posted since April 2015
(Reviewer's name in brackets)

April 2015

Mervyn Williams: From Modernism to the digital age, Edward Hanfling (Jodie Dalgleish)

Robert Ellis, Hamish Keith, Elizabeth Hana & Ngarino Ellis (Gregory O'Brien)

Richard Seddon, King of God's Own, Tom Brooking (Edmund Bohan)

Journey to a Hanging, Peter Wells (Max Oettli)

Passing Through, Coral Atkinson (Helen Watson White)

Si No Te Hubieras Ido / If Only You Hadn't Gone, Rogelio Guedea (Michael Harlow)

May 2015

you fit the description: The selected poems of Peter Olds (Richard Reeve)

PhotoForum at 40, Nina Seja (Gary Blackman)

MiStory, Philip Temple (Jack Ross)

The Children's Pond, Tina Shaw (David Herkt)

Working Lives c. 1900, Erik Olssen (James Dignan)

Puna Wai te Korero: An anthology of Māori poetry in English, Reina Whaitiri & Robert Sullivan (David Eggleton)

June 2015

Coal: The rise and fall of King Coal in New Zealand, Matthew Wright (Jeffrey Paparoa Holman)

Tragedy at Pike River: How and why 29 men died, Rebeccca McFie (Jeffrey Paparoa Holman)

Māori Boy: A memoir of childhood, Witi Ihimaera (Simone Oettli)

How Does it Hurt? Stephanie de Montalk (Michael Morrissey)

Lamplighter, Kerry Donovan Brown (Georgina McWhirter)

Reach, Laurence Fearnley (Chris Else)

A History of Contemporary Jewellery in Australia and New Zealand, Damian Skinner & Kevin Murray (David Eggleton)

Fingers: Jewellery for Aotearoa New Zealand, Damian Skinner & Finn McCahon-Jones (David Eggleton)

July 2015

Song of the Ghost in the Machine, Roger Horrocks (John Geraets)

Crankhandle: Notebooks November 2010–June 2012, Alan Loney (John Geraets)

The Gold Leaves, Edward Jenner (William Direen)

photosynthesis, Iain Britton (Jan Kemp)

The Holloway Press, 1994–2013, Francis McWhannell (Peter Vangioni)

Fred Graham: Creator of Forms – Te Tohunga Auaha, Maria de Jong (Damian Skinner)

Parekura Horomia – 'Kia Ora Chief', Wira Gardiner (Michael O'Leary)

August 2015

I, Clodia, and Other Portraits, Anna Jackson (John Horrocks)

Conversation by Owl-Light, Alexandra Fraser (John Horrocks)

Fallen Grace, MaryJane Thomson (John Horrocks)

The Facts of Light, Stephanie Christie (Robert McLean)

Headwinds, Lindsay Pope (Robert McLean)

Coracle, Peter Stuart (Robert McLean)

A Clearer View of the Hinterland, Jack Ross (Robert McLean)

The Breathing Tree, Apirana Taylor (Lindsay Rabbitt)

The Conch Trumpet, David Eggleton (Lindsay Rabbitt)

Mr Clean and the Junkie, Jennifer Compton (Natasha Dennerstein)

Bullet Hole Riddle, Miriam Barr (Natasha Dennerstein)

Real Fake White Dirt, Jess Holly Bates (Natasha Dennerstein)

Half Dark, Harry Ricketts (Vaughan Rapatahana)

Young Country, Kerry Hines (Vaughan Rapatahana)

Wonky Optics, Geoff Cochrane (Denys Trussell)

A Little Book of Sonnets, Julie Leibrich (Denys Trussell)

Driving With Neruda to the Fish'n'Chips, Leonel Alvarado (Denys Trussell)

September 2015

Hocken: Prince of Collectors, by Donald Kerr (Iain Sharp)

The Night We Ate the Baby, Tim Upperton (Michael Steven)

Only One Question, Tom Weston (Michael Steven)

In the Neighbourhood of Fame, Bridget van der Zijpp (Emily Brookes)

New Hokkaido, James McNaughton (James Dignan)

The Legend of Winstone Blackhat, Tanya Moir (Tasha Haines)

Greatest Hits, David Cohen (David Herkt)

POETRY

To Speak in Your Own Words in Your Own Voice

by Peter Simpson

Selected Poems by Charles Brasch, chosen by Alan Roddick (Otago University Press, 2015), 152 pp, $35

This book has been a long time coming. It is more than 40 years since Charles Brasch died in 1973, and more than 30 since his *Collected Poems*, also edited by Alan Roddick, appeared in 1984. Brasch is a fine and currently undervalued poet. It is good to have his work readily available in an intelligently chosen, well-presented selection. The cover painting by Max Gimblett (a great admirer of the poet's work) is an apt and bold choice. All six of Brasch's slim volumes were dressed in the discreet garments of Caxton Press's elegant and refined typography. It is no bad thing to present his work to new (and old) readers in a different, up-to-date format.

There is an orderly progression about Brasch's poetic career, governing both its outward signposts and its inward development. He published a similar-sized slim volume every decade or so: *The Land and the People* (1939), *Disputed Ground* (1948), *The Estate* (1957), *Ambulando* (1964), *Not Far Off* (1969), *Home Ground* (1974)—a book (or books in the case of the 1960s) in each of five decades from the 1930s to the 1970s. Read sequentially, Brasch's carefully chosen titles construct a kind of narrative: the figure of a man walking across a landscape ('ambulando'), tall and thin, as in a Giacometti sculpture—a journey from recognition of origins (land and people), through dispute about and accommodation to the terms of existence, to approach and arrival at a destination, home ground. Brasch's poetic journey has a satisfying coherence and completeness, reminiscent of T.S. Eliot's 'We shall not cease from exploration/ And the end of all our exploring/ Will be to arrive where we started/ And know the place for the first time' ('Little Gidding').

Roddick has selected from all six books, adding one poem, 'Man of Words', as a kind of foreword to the book ('these words I trace in dust and leave/ For others in their day to bear and live'), from 45 previously unpublished poems included in *Collected Poems* (Oxford University Press, 1984). That collection contained 198 poems; *The Land and the People* had 21, *Disputed Ground* also 21; *The Estate* had 19; *Ambulando* had 21; *Not Far Off* was much the largest with 45; in *Home Ground* there were 26. These figures relate to separate titles. If numbered parts of poems are counted as well the grand total comes close to well over 350. Roddick has selected something less than a third of this number, a total of 64 titles, or, if multiple parts are counted, 101.

The books Roddick favours most in his selections are the third, *The Estate* (1957) and the sixth, *Home Ground* (1974). He puts the emphasis firmly on the mature poet rather than on the early poems often selected by anthologists, which focus on matters of nationality. For instance Allen Curnow in his 1960 Penguin anthology took nine of 12 poems from the first two books, and, as recently as 2012, Stafford and Williams in the AUP anthology represented Brasch only by three poems written before 1945.

The Land and the People takes its title from a four-part poem (of which Roddick chooses two), which is Brasch's first attempt to articulate his and the nation's predicament. In language closely echoed by other writers of his generation, especially Curnow and Holcroft, Brasch writes of the land in largely negative terms:

> There are no dead in this land,
> No personal sweetness in its earth ... (p. 28)

Living in England from the age of 17, Brasch found that the impulse towards poetry was mostly stimulated by memories of home and thoughts about his native land, particularly after a return visit in 1938. The best of these early poems focus less on cultural reflections than on specifics of landscapes remembered or revisited, such as 'Pipikariti' and 'Waianakarua', both originally published in the Christchurch magazine *Tomorrow*.

> Only the thorn
> Alone on the parched rise, inhuman
>   matakauri
> Dry-green and fibrous, sorrowing,
> The gum-trees that offer their flower, their
>   sweet fruit
> Lightly to the bright and dangerous wind ...
>   (p. 27)

Such thorny particulars checked Brasch's penchant for shadowy (a favourite word) abstractions.

Disputed Ground was published after Brasch's return to New Zealand in 1946 but contains poems written during the war years, which were spent in England. As he explained in *Indirections* (1980), his posthumous autobiography, the outbreak of war stimulated him to write a number of poems about his homeland, 'now threatened also, with everything and everybody I knew' (p. 343). 'The Islands', originally three sonnets later reduced to a 10-line fragment, brought Brasch his first recognition in England; it was published by John Lehmann in *Penguin New Writing* 9, alongside work by Graham Greene, Cecil Day Lewis and Stephen Spender. Other pieces— 'A View of Rangitoto', 'Great Sea' and 'Forerunners'—were seized by Curnow for his Caxton anthology in 1945, contributing eloquently to his thesis that the poet is 'as the nerve to the body of his race, feeling and declaring the need or sickness which all suffer' (p. 46). Roddick rescues from oblivion 'Soldier in Reverie', a meditation on wartime 'anonymity' and 'incoherence', but the best of these poems is probably 'In Memory of Robin Hyde 1906–39'. Brasch, who befriended Hyde in

England, sees her—like Mark Gertler the painter and Ernst Toller the playwright, who also committed suicide that year—as a victim of the times, that 'low dishonest decade', as Auden called it:

> By choice you stood always on disputed
>   ground,
> At the utmost edge of life,
> Gazing into the firepit of disintegration
> Whose lavas threaten our small inherited
>   fields ... (p. 42)

The 1957 volume The Estate, containing the poems written after Brasch's return, is dominated by its title poem in 34 parts addressed to his friend T.H. (Harry) Scott, who later (1960) died in a mountaineering accident, an event the possibility of which haunts the poem:

> What have you seen on the summits, the
>   peaks that plunge their
> Icy heads into space? What draws you
>   trembling
> To blind altars of rock where man cannot
>   linger
> Even in death ... (xxiv, p. 73)

'The Estate' does not please everybody. Kendrick Smithyman, I recall, in a review in Here & Now, was embarrassed by its intimacy, associating it with a kind of 'adolescent crush' (if I remember rightly), but in truth that probably says as much about Smithyman's hard-nosed machismo as it does about Brasch. Curnow in a Press review calls The Estate 'one of the half-dozen or fewer really important books of New Zealand poetry of the last ten years'. Roddick would seem to agree, selecting 14 of the title poem's 34 sections for inclusion as well 11 shorter poems.

Particularly impressive are the sections of 'The Estate' in which Brasch addresses (anonymously) admired younger or older contemporaries; painter Colin McCahon, writers Noel Ginn and G.R. Gilbert, and composer Douglas Lilburn in section iii ('I think of your generation as the youngest/ That has found itself ...'), and Ursula Bethell in section xviii, especially her uncanny capacity to draw around her the talented young:

>   a dispersion, a murmuration
> Of spirits drawn by her wind-flung word and
>   offering
> Homage, asking for strength;
> Who formed a faint galaxy far about her ...
>   (p. 72)

Of the shorter poems from The Estate, 'The Ruins' and 'Autumn, Thurlby Domain' possess a Yeatsian amplitude and assurance, while 'Self to Self' has a sinewy strength reminiscent of Robert Graves, which anticipates Brasch's later style. Among this group I especially enjoyed 'Rest on the Flight into Egypt', an unusual poem in Brasch's output in that it locates a biblical story in a New Zealand setting, much as McCahon placed biblical events in local landscapes in his controversial early paintings (for which Brasch did much to gain acceptance). Reading recently through Brasch's journals of the 1950s I discovered the source of this poem in a picnic Brasch shared with friends on Otago Peninsula:

> And the mother holds him lightly, half
>   smiling, half aware
> Of mermaid grass springing fresh among
>   rocks

Ancient with silvered lichens, and of the air
Of late afternoon that, free and flowing on
From hill to hill, lapping the farthest
    headlands,
Gathers height and valley and distant
    township
And farm and bay below
And insect trawler crossing plains of sea
Into one picture and one world with her
Who has no world
Except the infant at her breast, husband
    beside her ... (p. 63)

Ambulando (1964) registers a marked turning inwards of Brasch's poetry, a turn especially evident in the title poem. Brasch was in his fifties when this book was published and the poems show an acute consciousness of ageing:

Now that the young with interest no longer
Look on me as one of themselves
Whom they might like to know or to touch,
Seeing merely another sapless greyhead,
The prospect of that disguise conducts me
Through any company unquestioned,
In cool freedom to come and go
With mode and movement, wave and wind.
    (p. 81)

Most surprising in this volume is a 'song cycle' (so-called by Brasch), 'In Your Presence'. These short love poems in regular stanzas range from two to 24 lines, and are remarkable for their quasi-metaphysical intensity, which is surprising given Brasch's normally reticent and measured tone. This piece (complete) is exemplary of their quality and character:

Buddleia for its scent in August,
Honey barb stinging the dusk,
I prize, and for that fume of anguish
Your love lends it, your severing love.

White cold star splitting the dusk,
Sweetness that searches nerve and soul
With blades of ice, and you, descended,
Stabbing my heart with lightning love. (p. 87)

In 1966 Brasch gave up editing *Landfall* after 'twenty years hard'. Presumably this gave him more time to write his own verse because his next book, *Not Far Off* (1969), his largest collection, followed only five years after *Ambulando*. There are, though, fewer stand-out poems than usual, in my view. 'Ode in Grey' is a moving if somewhat attenuated poem addressed to Johannes Bobrowski, an East German poet whom Brasch admired; 'Signals' is a rare expression of erotic sensuality; 'Man Missing' is a devastating analysis in short rhyming couplets of Brasch's sense of himself as 'a genuinely missing no-man' (p. 105). Probably the book's strongest poem is 'Chantecler', powerfully rhythmical, expertly rhymed, and remarkable for the intermittent savagery of its tone, somewhat reminiscent of Yeats' 'wild old wicked man' poems:

To see your neighbour as yourself
His heart stripped self-naked
Is to confess in every heart
The hateful and the crooked
Beneath its lies and boasting,
And at the roots of hate
The trivial and vapid. (p. 111)

Roddick selects only four of the poem's 13 sections, but it needs to be read in full to experience the full range of moods it offers.

Dead from cancer at 65, Brasch wrote strongly until the end of his life; indeed, the exquisite lyric 'Winter Anemones' was written within three weeks of his death. Not all poets of his generation in New Zealand ended so well; Mason, Fairburn, Glover, Dowling, Spear all faded as poets well before their end. But Brasch, like Curnow, sustained both quality and quantity of poetic output. *Home Ground*, published posthumously in 1974, was in preparation when he died. 'Shoriken', in 16 parts, is superb, its governing conceit of crossing the ocean balanced on the edge of his sword, derived from the sixteenth-century Japanese artist Motonobu, is wonderfully sustained:

> To speak in your own words in your own
> voice—
> How easy it sounds and how hard it is
> When nothing that is yours is yours alone
>
> To walk strongly yourself who are thousands
> Through all that made and makes you day
> by day
> To be and to be nothing, not to own
>
> Not owned, but lightly on the sword keep
> A dancer's figure—that is the wind's art
> With you who are blood and water, wind and
> stone. (p. 117)

'Home Ground', from which Roddick selects generously, comes as a genuine climax and summation, achieving a mood of acceptance and reconciliation that is very moving, as in the poem's smallest section, xiv:

> Silence will not let him go
> Entirely; allowed a few notes
> At the edge of dusk
> He will be recalled before long
> And folded into rock
> Reassumed by the living stream. (p. 127)

These days Brasch tends to be known better as an editor, collector, patron, friend and cultural benefactor than as a poet, but for him poetry always came first; it was his vocation and raison d'être. This fine selection of his best work should do much to give his poetry again the priority he accorded it himself.

Our Bright Eyes

by Lynley Edmeades

How to be Dead in a Year of Snakes, by
Chris Tse (AUP, 2014), 80 pp, $24.99

Whale Years, by Gregory O'Brien (AUP, 2015),
104 pp, $27.99

Two recent books from Auckland
University Press showcase both emerging
and veteran talent of New Zealand poetry.
Strong themes form the backbone of
these two books: *How to be Dead in a Year of
Snakes* reimagines a historical event in
Wellington in 1905; *Whale Years* explores
the South Pacific and its relation to New
Zealand. Both books are intriguing and
empathetic, and they invigorate imagined
and non-fictional dramas with poetic
skill and integrity.

Tse's debut collection interrogates the
death of Joe Kum Yung, a Chinese man
killed in 1905 in Wellington. Joe was shot
dead by a man called Lionel Terry, who,
according to historical accounts, thought
he was doing a service to the community
by eradicating the 'yellow peril'. While
Terry features at several points
throughout the book—as the xenophobic
antagonist—he is brought in as a prop to
explore the victim's world. Joe's life and
his place in cultural and ancestral
memory form the substance of the book-
length rumination, giving Tse a space to
take on the task of speaking for the
victim.

The first poem is a prose piece entitled
'In which the author interviews a dead
man'. This opening creates an air of
mystery from the outset: we're already in
the thick of the drama:

> No one asked me speak, nor took the time to
> fill a moment with my presence. We cannot
> hide from ourselves in the dark. I crouch
> down in the damp void and listen as they pass
> words about me between themselves like
> borrowed scandal. The loudest, hungriest
> voices drown out all reason.

From here we are taken back to 1871,
to the victim's 'first impressions' of this
'unsettling' country: 'how its generosity/
of space is inflicted upon our bright
eyes'. These 'bright eyes', it transpires,
are those of the immigrant Chinese who
came to New Zealand in hope of finding
wealth and fortune. A hundred years on,
we readers know the often sad reality of
these dreams, and Tse explores this
bitter-sweetness through the use of
ghosts (in 'Eight Ghosts'), Māori
mythology and customs ('kawe mate', 'te
rerenga wairua'), and the mention of
historical events, such as the sinking of
SS *Ventnor*.[1]

Having met the victim, we soon meet
his murderer, and are thrust into the
event itself: '1905: this is the end'. And
yet this is just the beginning, as the old
cliché goes; the rest of the book then
meanders through the consequences of
the murder, historically and
imaginatively. As these meditations
continue, so too do the tropes and hooks
that tie the thing together: voices,
whisperings, shadows, snakes, secrets,

and the possibility of giving the voiceless a mouth through which to speak. One particular moment seems to encapsulate these utterances:

> The heaviness of the years
> tests our defences and
> questions our beliefs
> so when pain is stretched
> across decades of silence
> a slip of the tongue could demolish
> entire histories.

There is an underlying anxiety that drives the collection: the sense that if poetry does not bring this tale back to life 'entire histories' could be 'demolished'. This urgency comes through in some of the formal experimentation, too, where Tse uses language to push off from itself. In a beautifully titled piece ('In Which the Author Interviews Light'), we again find voice and breath and light and shadow, this time used performatively:

If	I	could		speak
all	you'd	hear	is	echo
over				here
—	no,	over	here	—
—		there		—

It's a difficult thing to pull off, this book-length meditation on a historical event. The poet has to confront issues of repetition, possible sentimentality, narrative arcs and, perhaps above all else, the eradication of the poet's ego from the poems themselves. And yet Tse makes this look quite effortless. While each poem fits figuratively into its own place in the book's sequence, there are

moments where the poems work in their own right. There are some brief instances of unnecessary abstraction, where the poet runs the risk of losing the reader's attention, but these slips are few and relatively far between.

The themes of the book are hefty, rich and sometimes imposing: Chinese mythology, New Zealand settler history, ancestry and collective memory. But these themes are made alluring by being couched in layers of craftsmanship, formal experimentation and a kind of kaleidoscopic poetic play. The result is curious and original, not only illustrating some of the possibilities of the long poem or sequence, but also forging out new poetic treatments of the historical subject.

★

Gregory O'Brien is something of a household name in New Zealand arts and literature, and rightly so. His contribution to the arts, across many platforms, is vast and, by the looks of things, will not be slowing down any time soon. His most recent written output, *Whale Years*, sees the poet and artist following the migratory routes of whales and seabirds across large belts of the South Pacific, both literally and figuratively. The resulting collection is substantial, accomplished and luminous.

Not unlike Tse's collection, *Whale Years* also has strong themes that form the foundation of the book. However, rather than attempting to tell a victim's lost story (and thereby keeping the self at bay), the poet himself is much more present in this work. Along with themes of migration, mythologies and an existential enquiry of the human's place in a vast but troubled landscape, the poems also deal directly with where the poet fits into this scheme. The result of this presence is quite often a playful and curious participation with both familiar and foreign landscapes, a sense that the poet trusts his reader and is in some way confiding in us: 'with beaches I am often/ in agreement/ their slow/ shuffle, organizational/ skills' ('Oneraki'). And, from 'Luck Bird':

> My feast day an occasion of some solemnity.
> It arrives, as any other, by sea—my nesting place
> and vantage point, from where I behold
> this world's wonders—a black cat
>
> eating a cucumber, the magnetic navel
> of a woman, a boy with dog meat
> between his teeth ...

There is a trusting voice—the poet wants to tell us what he sees, thinks and feels. But there is also a trusting skill, whereby he knows his craft so well he does not need to force it upon us. It is clear we are in the hands of a poet who knows his trade, and he is having fun with his material.

Behind the curious eye that leads the poet to glance at all of these things there is also an eye for the quirks: some of the more surreal details that often go unnoticed. Some things come up again and again—like balloons—with which the poet performs a kind of dance. We meet the balloon early, on page 13, in 'Weather Balloon, Raoul Island', a kooky little meditation on an equally kooky phenomenon: every day at 10.30 am, since 1940 no less, a weather balloon is released by Department of Conservation workers on Raoul Island. The balloon never returns, but explodes in mid-air after issuing valuable weather information back down to land, 'to transmit back to us/ immensities, unimaginable/ altitudes, the intelligence/ of ages'. The result is interesting, but without the help of Google, the piece itself seems a little flimsy. However, what is more compelling is the continual return of said balloon throughout the rest of the book. The piece that follows directly, 'The Loneliness of the Raoul Island Weather Balloon' is an absolute delight:

> weather balloon
> whether balloon
> whenever balloon
> whether we goest and from
>   whence we come balloon
> whither balloon
> with-her balloon
>   without-her balloon
> wither balloon

The poems travel from the Chathams to the Kermadecs, from Tonga to Chile, from Waihi to Waiheke, from Raoul Island to Rapanui (or Easter Island), and quite often the balloon does too (a later poem is titled 'Conversation between a stone head on Easter Island and the weather balloon, Raoul Island').

The last of the three sections of the book is a kind of homecoming. In

'Memory of a Fish' the poet addresses his son Felix, who has recently returned from the Kermadec Islands. This is an epic of sorts, a 16-page rumination on journeys—the poet's own and his son's—in an increasingly precarious world. While its compact three-line stanzas (which tilt and turn as a kind of textual homage to the sea, perhaps) often lose tack with some jarring line breaks, the final result is ambitious, seamless and remarkably unsentimental. It signs off the collection with a beautiful story about a man being reunited with a giant groper after 50 years to find that the fish remembers him. The poem's title takes on new meaning.

Such is O'Brien's way. His poetry resists being this or that, but opts instead for a mysterious in-between, whereby he invites his reader to come and play with him, in language, history and the mysticism of our own South Pacific heritage. O'Brien draws lines between points where many mythologies have long ceased to exist, and he does so with the imprint of a fine craftsman.

---

1 The SS *Ventnor* set out for China with the bones of 499 Chinese men who had died in New Zealand. The ship hit a rock off the Taranaki coast and sank in the Hokianga Harbour. Some bones were washed up on shore and local Māori tribes buried them with their own people.

The Unclosed Door
by Alice Miller

Otherwise, by John Dennison (AUP), 60 pp, $29.99

Like Seamus Heaney, John Dennison loves his Anglo-Saxon monosyllables, as in the excellent sonnet 'Crookes' Radiometer', which begins:

> Hand-blown: how clear things become
> pushed near to breaking point, breath
> in the hot glob of dust: the bright form
> of the skull.

In this passage, the only time Dennison breaks into polysyllables is with the verbs *become* and *breaking*, and the only Latinate words are *clear*, *pushed*, *point*. But as the radiometer starts to move, the diction too shifts, until we reach 'utter answerability', 'scintilla' and 'silicate hymn'. We are moving between earth and the ethereal.

Dennison plays language like an instrument; these poems frequently emphasise or ironise their content by manipulating rhythm, sound, diction and syntax. They adhere to and break away from traditional form, or alternate between formal and colloquial language in order to propel a poem towards change or revelation. Many of the poems embrace or flirt with traditional forms; Dennison is particularly keen on a loose Shakespearean sonnet, sometimes omitting the rhyme scheme, sometimes adhering with half-rhyme, occasionally adopting a rhyme scheme of his own.

The prosody is also worth noticing; we might scan the following fragment like this:

```
-  /   /  -   /   -  /  -   /
so that, having passed, we labour with

-   /   -  /   -   / -  /   -   /
  -
the air, with balance—any progress this way

-   /   /   /   /   /
is hard-fought, self-won, wrath ...
    (Ecce, III)
```

Look at how the iambic and trochaic feet of the first and second lines (which refer to 'balance' and 'progress') give way to the heavily stressed 'hard-fought, self-won, wrath' in the third line. He is making his music work. These are serious poems, but they are, crucially, not averse to play. Dennison's work is peppered with colloquialisms—'telly' for instance, and frequent use of the word 'wee'. (There is also an all-too-memorable poem about an explosive moment in a dunny.) In 'Sleepers', another sonnet, the poem opens with an earnest, level tone:

> Friends decide to separate. After,
> we enter the clearing, retrace our steps. A fine
> rain settles, and everything is un-
> accountably beautiful, unaccountable,
> being not promised ...

The poem goes on to describe the overgrown grass in the dirt, and the penultimate line raises the speaker's awkward interjection:

> We look down. *Gutted for you, mate.*

The rhythm and the tone are both 'gutted' at this point, along with the speaker's sentiment. We experience the gap between what's said and what's felt—not just the 'otherwise' of what we might say, but the 'otherwise' of the entire separation; if only, the form says, it had been different.

Colloquialisms are in full, joyous force at the beginning of 'After Geering', where the poem evokes a modern young person's vernacular:

> And we're like
> oh my *god* like
>
> it's so true like,
> he was saying:
>
> Life has become a venture?
> in which each of us is now responsible?
> for creating our own personal meaning
>   system?

Not only do we get the 'like', the glorious 'upspeak' ('a venture?', 'our own personal meaning system?'), and even the classic student word 'relatable', but as the poem continues, it twists, turns and reveals a very different tone:

> He was despised and rejected by others; a
>   man
> of suffering and acquainted with infirmity;
>   and like
>
> one from whom others hide their faces
> he was despised, and we held him of no
>   account.
>
> And he was poured out like
> water.

Dennison's poems often end with a movement— physical, tonal or a shift in attention. Final lines include: 'Step from the house into the garden'; 'Turn, heart, turn—go back home;/ leave this road unwound'; 'call the unseen guest to the potluck table'; '... profoundly moved towards home.'

Robert Frost said of the progress of a poem that it 'begins in delight and ends in wisdom'. In an echo of Yeats' wild swans, Dennison's substitutes geese:

> I watch them go, a dream of wing-beat and
>   assent
> beyond say-so, beyond call, and I long
>
> for the swoop and grab by the scruff of the
>   neck, the unquestioning,
>
>   unlooked-for lift out of this menagerie,
>
> this forsaken plot, the proving ground of
>   love.

The 'proving ground of love' is the setting for these poems. Dennison's is a universe that glimpses and tries to grasp certainty. One of the problems with New Zealand poetry can be a tendency towards the lightweight; there are books I have enjoyed in the moment, but once put down I've never felt compelled to pick them up again. This book asks for more. The epigraph announces the book's intention:

> Let us lay down then, lay down
> the copious, unmarked preserves
> of the squirrelling, querulous heart
>
> and return to gratitude—find
> the given in our homing,
> the word to end all boasting.

This collection, with its complex, generous poems, is itself a 'return to gratitude'. This intention, and the collection as a whole, do raise a question. Is it true what Tolstoy said about happy families? Is unhappiness more interesting? Don't we love the *Inferno*

more than the *Paradiso*?; don't we find Milton's Satan more compelling than his God? In *Otherwise* there are times when any imperilment feels very far away, particularly in poems like 'Promissory', or 'The Garden', the latter of which progresses by means of repeating particular phrases: 'light gathers in', 'now you walk', 'love speaks', 'a promise held open'.

The poem 'Lone Kauri (reprise)' appropriates not just Curnow, but Dylan Thomas's 'Rage, rage against the dying of the light', and John Donne's plea to the 'three-person'd God' to '[b]atter my heart', to 'break, blow, burn'—but Dennison's answer to all this is a calm reassurance:

> ... Forgive my making light of
> the glass half-empty and you weighing up
>   the dregs;
>
> but I will get up like a love-cast father
> awakening to children's voices, the night-
> time true underfoot, who hears their laughter
>
> and finds, at the unclosed door, the seam of
>   light.

And this is Dennison's project, the poetry of the love-cast father, where night-time is 'true underfoot', doors are unclosed, and through them, spill light.

People of the Land

By Jeffrey Paparoa Holman

Tangata Whenua: An illustrated history,
by Atholl Anderson, Judith Binney and Aroha Harris (Bridget Williams Books, 2014), 544pp, $99.99

In 1855 in London, two major studies of the original inhabitants of the distant colony of New Zealand were published: Governor George Grey's *Polynesian Mythology and Ancient Traditional History of the New Zealand Race as furnished by their Chiefs and Priests*, and the missionary Richard Taylor's *Te Ika a Maui: New Zealand and its inhabitants*. Here were two comprehensive attempts at a global history of Māori society by the twin colonising voices of a post-literate world: church and state. The pre-literate world of Māori oral tradition had entered the pages of modernity in what was the beginning of a written flood—fact, fiction and fancy that has continued to the present, from the modern to the postmodern, from treaty signing to treaty breaches and treaty settlements. *Tangata Whenua: An illustrated history*, with its six contributors, is the latest to enter the list of what has proved to be an enduring literary genre: locating Māori in time, place and print.

Weighing in at over 500 pages—truly a book that might be best read standing at a pulpit, such is its bulk—it is a sumptuous artefact to which the description 'lavishly illustrated' seems faint praise indeed. The publishers, those champions of New Zealand intellectual life, Bridget Williams Books, have spared no expense in producing this work, supported by an impressive array of benefactors, keeping the price down to a remarkable $100 worth of information, argument, artwork, photography, maps and diagrams, all reproduced on high-quality paper and stoutly bound. What matters most, however, is its respect for its subject and the inherent mana of the story: first peoples, tangata whenua, people of the land, te iwi Māori. Not that Pākehā do not figure—they could not be excluded—but the book is exactly focused on Māori stories and world views; although three of the six contributors happen to be Pākehā, it is still their brief to bring what Māori were doing and saying to the fore.

The book divides into three main sections, roughly speaking: the pre-contact era, then the nineteenth and twentieth centuries, with some overlap. The familiar categories—Te Ao Tawhito, Te Ao Hou and Te Ao Hurihuri—structure the narrative where the writers create their weaving. Ngāi Tahu historian and anthropologist Atholl Anderson covers the material origins from 3000 BC and histories up until 1830; historians Judith Binney, Vincent O'Malley and Alan Ward from the arrival of Pākehā to the post-Land War years of recovery up until

1920; while historians Aroha Harris (Te Rarawa, Ngāpuhi) and Melissa Matutina Williams (Te Rarawa, Ngāti Maru) take the reader from the inter-war years through 1945 and beyond into the era of renaissance and today's post-settlement era. Each of the chapters in these sections is bookended with two-page *Across Time* sequences, often from guest contributors, that look more closely at topics covered in the general sweep of the previous narrative.

The whole impression is of a judicious choice of history makers and designers with the aim of producing a book having enough heft to satisfy the academic community from which the writers emerge, yet beautiful and compelling enough in its visual storytelling to make the world described and analysed come alive in the reader's hands. There will be those who take issue with one or the other of specialist areas covered—how could there not be—but the right balance has been struck here, in making available the latest research and argument brought to the fore in the post-settlement era (in the case of much recent iwi history making, fed by the Waitangi Tribunal casebook of reports). There are any number of specialist studies available now in the wake of the baby-boom and post-baby-boom historians' works, as a fresh crop of doctorates have entered the field looking for subjects in need of revision, or examination for the first time.

That is not what this book is about, however; some of these writers are here,

others not, but what really matters is for whom this massive work is intended and whom it reaches. Clearly, while written by specialists, it is not targeted at other specialists: it is part of a nation-building project, as were the two works mentioned earlier, written by Europeans with their feet on the land but their hearts and minds shaped by England and a Eurocentric tradition. This time the view is from here, by here, to here; the historiography may be Western, but the book is a Pacific production, inconceivable elsewhere and meant primarily for its country of origin and its people, first comers and late. There is hardly a page that lacks an artefact, a face, a figure, a carving, a painting that could only have come from Aotearoa and its tangata whenua, te iwi Māori.

Whether we are looking at the carved doors of kumara storage pits from Opotiki, the burning of the pā buildings at Orakei in 1950, Hinewehi Mohi performing the song 'Kotahitanga' in a still from a video made in Epping Forest, or police commissioner Mike Bush stooping in a harirū (handshake) with a Ruātoki kuia as part of an apology he made over the Operation 8 police raids in the area in 2007, we are looking at a world made by Māori in which we all share. This is not a book all New Zealanders could afford, but one we cannot afford to miss. It needs to be in every library, every school, every kura and whare wānanga, in government offices and in every university in multiple copies; most of all it needs to be in every wharenui, on every marae and in the homes of those—Māori and Pākehā—who care about where we come from and where we might go from here.

It is also fitting to note—as do the authors in their introduction—that one of their number, Dame Judith Binney, died in 2011 before the book could be completed. Having delivered her magnum opus, a Tūhoe history *Encircled Lands*, to the iwi at Ruātoki in December 2009, she was honoured with the name 'Te Tomairangi o te Aroha' at Waikirikiri marae. The name holds the meaning 'the dew of love', a significant and enduring tribute from a people who, over their history, could find little to honour in their treatment at the hands of the Pākehā majority surrounding their papakainga, Te Urewera.

E te kaituhituhi rongonui, e te rangatira, haere, haere, haere atu rā!

Imperial Desire
by Paul Moon

Entanglements of Empire: Missionaries, Māori, and the question of the body, by Tony Ballantyne (AUP, 2015), 378 pp, $40

The great histories of the British encounters with New Zealand, including those of Alan Ward, James Belich and Anne Salmond, together with the meticulous accounts of early missionary activity in the country, particularly the studies by Judith Binney, John Stenhouse, Allan Davidson and Peter Lineham, have left New Zealand well served with analyses of evangelical activity in the country in the early nineteenth century. Is there anything substantially new to be added, then, to the fairly exhaustively examination of this field?

Tony Ballantyne's *Entanglements of Empire* offers a resounding 'yes' to this question. Inevitably, he treads much of the ground already traversed by other historians, and there are few surprises as he chronicles the motives and methods of the various players in the Protestant missionary movements as they prised New Zealand open to further the reach of their evangelising efforts in the region. However, as is the case throughout *Entanglements of Empire*, familiarity does not come across as repetitious. Indeed, even some of the best-known episodes of the era—such as Marsden's much-lionised first sermon in New Zealand on

Christmas Day 1814, or the growing trade between New Zealand and New South Wales in the 1820s—are illuminated in new ways, thanks to Ballantyne's mastery of various perspectives of British imperial dynamics (detailed in his 2012 book *Webs of Empire*), and to his preparedness to build on the current historiography of the era, drawing on other disciplines, ranging from economics to theology and sociology, to encourage the reader to look at the familiar in sometimes several alternative ways, and as part of larger frameworks of meaning. The result is that the social, political, economic, linguistic, cultural, gender, educational, technological and other changes that radiated from the work of the early Protestant missionaries in New Zealand are encompassed in this book.

This focus on perspective and interpretation is a central characteristic of *Entanglements of Empire*. Without ever looking for novelty for its own sake, or sounding laboured, Ballantyne excavates what we may think we know or think is commonplace, and in the process inevitably turns up nuggets of new insight and interpretation. The links between Marsden's civilisation mission and concepts of time, the role of power in William Yate's sexual transgressions, and the political consequences of the specific ways in which Māori were represented among missionaries in the 1820s and 1830s are just a few of the numerous ways in which this book breaks new ground in our understanding of this period of missionary activity in New Zealand. And throughout the work, Ballantyne advises the reader explicitly how these perspectives and interpretations build on the existing body of scholarship.

Given the considerable and growing range of research on the religious dimensions of colonialism, Ballantyne has had to navigate the tangle of terminology that has grown around the subject. Terms such as 'conversion', 'evangelisation', 'pagan', 'evil', 'righteousness' and even 'Christianity' are loaded with cultural and social as much as religious meanings, and Ballantyne has been concise and consistent in the way he has used such terms. None is left open to the reader's presumptions.

The genesis of British missionary involvement in New Zealand extends back to Christ's instruction to his disciples to spread his message throughout the world (Matthew 28: 16– 20). In the case of British Protestant missionary activity from the 1810s through to the close of the 1830s, New Zealand was one of the newest fields of Christian proselytising, and when these missionaries encountered Māori during this era there was confusion and chafing as much as comprehension and conciliation. It is the character, motives, manifestations and consequences of these encounters that form the basis of this book.

Entanglements of Empire is divided into six large chapters, each of which commences with a general contention that Ballantyne intends to explore. The first chapter—'Exploration, empire, and evangelization'—serves initially as a scene-setter. However, even at this early stage Ballantyne has already pulled out his historical lens, and has the reader looking at engagements between Europeans and Māori in the context of what he calls 'imperial desire'. This is the framework for British evangelical thought and activity in the region, culminating with Marsden's plans for New Zealand—plans which Ballantyne demonstrates depended strongly on existing commercial, political, cultural, linguistic and other networks in the region. It is at this juncture that Ballantyne explores the confluence of imperial history and Māori history. Each of these histories is a necessary counterpoint to the other, but in the eyes of Marsden and most of his missionary contemporaries, their pursuit of the 'civilisation' project obscured their perception of Māori history and culture in ways that were to have repercussions on the mission for decades.

'Marking place, reordering space' is the next chapter, and is where Ballantyne's expansive analysis begins to open up. He explores the concept of mission stations as places of everyday activity as well as centres of Christianity and therefore fulfilling symbolic as well as temporal roles. He addresses the marginalisation of Māori in many missionary accounts of the establishment of Christianity, and in the course of this accords Māori agency the recognition it often failed to receive in the minds of Europeans of this period. Ngāpuhi chief Ruatara's domination over the country's first mission station, and the way in which missionaries were unwittingly woven into hapū and iwi politics, is detailed by Ballantyne, as is the declining significance of chiefly patronage in the following decade.

The reader is reminded in this chapter that little is ever culturally neutral in imperial/religious encounters; Ballantyne imbues something as seemingly innocuous as a missionary house with a new set of meanings. Elements of space, domesticity, tapu, gender, education, hygiene and, importantly, individualised property rights are brought together and examined initially as individual topics, and then for their cumulative effects on the nature of Protestant missionary activity, and for the Māori responses to them.

The third chapter, 'Economics, labor, and time', surveys the extent to which the missionaries' urge to civilise Māori extended into the realm of time, as they 'struggled to dislodge traditional [Māori] rhythms of work'. The arguments here are compelling, although possibly more consideration could have been given to the influence of traders and the very secular demands of the trans-Tasman market, particularly as patterns of Māori economic activity evolved in remarkably similar ways in places where there was no missionary presence.

There is, in this chapter, a puzzling translation of Te Atua Wera as 'the burned god'. Typically, Ngāpuhi (followed by Binney) have translated Te Atua Wera as 'the fiery god' or 'the fire god', which has rather different connotations. Polack's intriguing account of the origins of the Nakahi sect could also have been included in this analysis, as well as some of the Ngāpuhi oral histories of the sect, as they point to Nakahi being founded on more dubious grounds than some of the other fusion religions of the nineteenth century.

The focus on the body is more pronounced in the fourth chapter, 'Containing transgression', where the Christian ideals of sexual restraint were (perhaps inevitably, given the experience of missionary activity in other parts of the Empire) violated by some of the New Zealand missionaries. The accusations made against Yate—that he had relationships with a number of young Māori men and boys—are considered in the setting of 'the overlapping webs of relationships that he fashioned', which include considering how the scandal around Yate's activities was, to some degree, 'shaped by the broader social dynamics and conflicts that he set in motion'. The repercussions of Yate's actions extended to the whole of the missionary community in New Zealand at the time and, along with other moral transgressions, dented mission morale.

'Cultures of death', the penultimate chapter, offers a fascinating insight into how Māori ideas of death sometimes collided and sometimes were a point of commonality with those held by early nineteenth-century evangelical British missionaries. Ballantyne describes the subject of death as 'a crucial window for both missionaries and Māori into each other's worlds'. Not just a window, but sometimes also a door through which one culture could step into the domain of the other. When the chief Ruatara was dying he was declared tapu and only tohunga could approach him. Yet missionary Thomas Kendall was allowed to enter Ruatara's presence, where he attempted (unsuccessfully) a deathbed conversion. Ballantyne also observes that in rituals such as burials, place and culture modified conventional practices among Europeans in some instances. Death was one of the realms where cultural collusion was at its greatest between Protestant missionaries and Māori communities from the 1810s to the 1830s.

The final chapter of *Entanglements of Empire*, 'The politics of the "enfeebled" body', offers a textual analysis of sources that fall into the category of 'humanitarian narratives', which 'focused on the sufferings of another's body in order to engender compassion and to urge ameliorative action'. Ballantyne demonstrates how these narratives played an important role in the development of British policy on New Zealand in the 1830s, casting the incremental acts of British intervention in the light of an ongoing response to a humanitarian concern.

In addition to Ballantyne's approach to his subject matter, two features that further elevate this book are its very clear prose style and the tight control of the way in which primary source material is used and presented. A work approaching 400 pages devoted to one group of missionaries operating in small pockets of a sparsely inhabited territory over just a few decades could suggest the inclusion of superfluous detail, or excessive diversions into areas of analysis only loosely connected with the main topic. However, Ballantyne maintains a strong discipline throughout. The material is clearly structured, the prose is taut, and the meaning always clear. And despite the inevitably contrapuntal nature of the way in which concepts and historical content are conveyed, these always end in a clear resolution.

The much more significant triumph of *Entanglements of Empire*, though, is the way in which the array of ideas and perspectives Ballantyne offers the reader is incorporated seamlessly into the extensive history laid out in the book. Moreover, the themes raised are sometimes built on in subsequent parts of the book, rather than being rigidly compartmentalised in their respective chapters.

To my knowledge, there is no other volume on this period of New Zealand history that addresses the character of Protestant missionary activity from such a range of perspectives, or with the sheer weight of erudition that Ballantyne brings to this book. *Entanglements of Empire* is a work of international significance in the field of nineteenth-century British imperialism, and worthy of the highest praise for the way in which it not just advances, but in many instances recalibrates our understanding of this vital period in New Zealand's colonial history.

The Truth of Music
by William Dart

Memories of Early Years and Other Writings,
by Douglas Lilburn, ed. Robert Hoskins
(Steele Roberts, 2014), $39.99

Introducing a new collection of Douglas Lilburn's writings, *Memories of Early Years*, editor Robert Hoskins stresses the importance of the land to the New Zealand composer. Within a few paragraphs he quotes from *Search for a Tradition*, Lilburn's seminal 1946 address to the First Cambridge Music School, which is receiving its third publication as part of this book:

> I feel that a musician in this country must develop his awareness of the place he lives in, not attempting a mere imitation of nature in sound, but seeking its inner values, the manifestations of beauty and purpose it shows us from time to time, and perhaps using it as something against which he can test the validity of his own work.

Hoskins, in fact, launches his introduction with a selection of vivid images locating the young Lilburn in the Rangitikei land around him. We see the boy catching eels and chasing turkeys in the country, getting spooked in the bush and, extraordinarily, daubing his face with glow-worms to create warpaint for playing Tarzan and Deerfoot. By the end of these introductory pages, Hoskins has moved to more inherently musical issues. He draws parallels between the mysterious 'night music' of the Hungarian composer Béla Bartók and the eco-shimmer of Lilburn's last electronic work, *Soundscape with Lake and River*.

The 43 pages of Lilburn's long essay 'Memories of early years', which gives the book its title, are published for the first time. Exquisitely sketched, they are imbued with the same sense of rural nostalgia that Bruce Mason would later bring to Takapuna Beach in *The End of the Golden Weather*. This is a charmed, privileged and sometimes isolated childhood caught in potent and pithy snapshots by the elderly composer in the late 1980s.

Inevitably, we look for clues here as to the forces that shaped the later Lilburn, just as the Danish composer Carl Nielsen (1865–1931) reveals so much of his make-up in his 1927 memoir *Min Fynske Barndom*, which Lilburn knew and admired through its 1953 translation as *My Childhood*. The Nielsen book is a substantial piece of writing, dealing out primal, dramatic images. We meet young Carl lying in a big pool of water, laughingly unaware of peril and saved from drowning by the check linsey-woolsey frock he is wearing. After this averted tragedy, he fashions a whole paragraph around suckling at his mother's bare breast.

Encounters are not so earthy in Lilburn's earliest memories. He recalls grasping at the brass buttons on his oldest brother's army uniform as they glisten in the sunlight, although there are threats of danger here, too, when he topples a vessel of scalding water. Early on his mother sings him 'The Swallows', a drawing-room ballad by the Victorian composer Frederic H. Cowen. 'Only many years later,' Lilburn remembers, 'did I realize that we had no swallows at Drysdale, and this left a recurring question about the truth of music as related to experience.' At first the musical art 'remained in some curiously baffling vacuum, and I gained no systematic basic techniques of performance'.

Isolated, with no radio even to bring a range of music into the household, he recalls his sister, Janet, persuading their mother to buy her an HMV portable gramophone 'to indulge an adolescent passion for pop hits of the day, and requited her by mooning about the house singing "Hallelujah I'm a Bum".' It is a scene that cries out to be caught on celluloid; even more so when the young Lilburn takes her side and 'gladly joined her in the incipient revolt, while mother complained: "Why don't you sing some good hymns?"'

With these writings, there is the fascination of assessing someone else's bookshelves or CD collections, especially when there is talk of his first musical encounters. A 'weird version' of The [sic] Messiah is reported on, and among the family record collection we have 'Wurlitzer organ stunners' by Albert Ketelby and, relics of more innocent times, George Moran and Charles E. Mack's blackface vaudeville act, Two Black Crows.

Towards the end of Lilburn's reminiscences there is a piece of writing that catches this musician's feeling for the land, along with a tang of incipient homoeroticism, and the eternal problem of finding a suitably vernacular tone in singing the composer's Denis Glover song-cycle Sings Harry:

> In my later experience I remember it also for hearing 'Just [sic] singing in the rain' from the rough tenor voice of lead shepherd Lionel Park, vigorous immediate and formative sound matching the panorama from a high ridge with a vast view and the friendship and health of young exercise that I was discovering. Music and experience began to relate to each other in some intuitive way.

Of the three addresses printed here, the Cambridge one, 'A search for tradition', is an essential cultural document. Here is a young composer trying to find an individual and relevant voice on the other side of the world from the Europe he had always looked to. Many of his comments are startlingly prescient. Most valuable here is Hoskins' access to original documentation for this, and Lilburn's 1969 'A search for a language', showing fascinating emendations to the original text, by both the composer himself and editor John Mansfield Thomson.

There's a homely charm to Lilburn's additional sentence, after a discussion of New Zealand intellectuals who remain locked in Europe. 'I don't altogether blame them because whenever I buy a New Zealand-made shirt for instance, I find the buttons have a tendency to fall off the second time I put it on, and, perhaps, to stretch the image a little, the buttons are always falling off.'

Appearing for the first time in this publication is 'A search for a sound', Lilburn's address on the launching of the Christchurch Society for Contemporary Music in April 1967. The struggle of our composers to put the music of today in front of audiences is carefully charted. There is some bitterness here. Reacting to our country being rated as perfect by a Washington computer, he adds, '[W]e do not hear enough of what the imperfect rest of world is doing musically, and the situation is not likely to change unless we make some special initial effort in the most advanced musical thought of our times.'

Elsewhere he describes the revelations of hearing Bartók; however, by the 1950s he was experiencing John Ogdon playing Webern's 'Variations' from memory. A few years later his Victoria colleague Frederick Page goes to Darmstadt and brings back Stockhausen, Cage and Nono, meaning that Bartók, Schoenberg and Webern were 'relegated to history'.

The most revealing comment, vis-à-vis Lilburn's own music, comes when he describes his new interest in electroacoustic music as the opportunity to explore 'my own total heritage of sound, meaning all sounds, not just the narrow segments that we've long regarded as being music'.

He talks in detail on just one of his own works, his score for the Michael Forlong's 1950 film *Journey for Three*, dramatising the postwar government immigration scheme. Lilburn's commentary was written for a radio broadcast. Musical descriptions are aided by score extracts, and editor Hoskins rather quaintly footnotes the word 'pommie' as 'slang (usually disparaging) for English immigrant'.

There are three pieces on Ralph Vaughan Williams, his old teacher from the Royal College of Music; the most interesting is one written for the older composer's centennial in 1972, in which Lilburn admits that 'the past ten years I've grown away from listening to his music'.

A piece on Ravi Shankar—another radio broadcast—reveals both his openness of spirit (George Harrison and the Monterey Pop Festival are tagged) and takes care to credit the work of New Zealand pianist Dorothy Davies in bringing Indian music to this country.

Tributes to various friends and colleagues are warm and unaffected, and reflect the close-knit community in which Lilburn moved. An unpublished tribute to painter Evelyn Page is particularly fine, describing a 'sure development ... from apprentice study of smoky Rembrandts towards the glowing colours, exhilaration and rhythmic vitality of her later work'.

It seems churlish to find fault in such a beautifully produced book, featuring some key paintings by Evelyn Page and Rita Angus, as well as the published score of the 'Mountain Rescue' sequence from *Journey for Three*. However, the elusive Lilburn essay 'Elgar and radical bias', which appeared in the 22 July 1936 issue of the forward-thinking Christchurch periodical *Tomorrow*, and which was overlooked by Philip Norman in the first printing of his magnificent tome on the composer's life, could well have been included. The 29-year-old composer was emphatically not of the generation that Elgar represented, yet his assessment is remarkably level-headed and fair, with a concluding paragraph that might well be heeded by the young radicals of today.

> The radical is perhaps a little inclined to progress with his nose fast to the ground of social problems, to the neglect of ultimate artistic realities. He would do well to approach Elgar with an open mind until he can distinguish readily between the products of an imperialistic philosophy, and those of a fine artistic experience.

FICTION

Hot Stuff in the Wrong Way

by David Herkt

New Country: Plays and stories, by James Courage (Genre Press, 2015), 196 pp, $39.95

The first novel by a New Zealand writer to deal explicitly with the subject of homosexual desire between men was James Courage's *A Way of Love*, published in London in 1959 and banned in New Zealand in 1961. The word 'explicit' is important in this context. While Frank Sargeson's accounts of desire between men in stories like 'A Great Day' (1940) and 'That Summer' (1943) seem more than apparent to a contemporary reader, it is largely because the absence is the presence. The concealment of homosexual desire is often their motive, their method and, frequently, their subject. Courage's *A Way of Love*, on the other hand, has a self-proclaimed homosexual narrator, concerns a homosexual relationship, and is set in a homosexual milieu in London. Often it examines itself as a part of what we might now call 'Queer Literature'.

Courage was the author of eight novels, several plays and many short stories. Born in 1903 into a pastoral family, he spent his early childhood at

Seadown, a sheep station near Amberley in the South Island. He was educated in Christchurch, travelled to Britain, and graduated from St John's College, Oxford, with a BA in 1927. With the exception of a two-year period in New Zealand in the mid-1930s, he would spend the rest of his life in London working as a bookseller and a writer. In the words of the *Dictionary of New Zealand Biography*, he 'never married'.

A Way of Love is one of three Courage novels to be set entirely in Britain. A 49-year-old bachelor and architect, Bruce Quantock, attends a winter performance of a Schubert symphony in London's Festival Hall where he accidentally steps on a woman's fur coat, then collides with a young man's head as they bend simultaneously to pick it up. His thoughts full of the encounter, Bruce continues on to the all-male party that introduces the reader to a specific postwar British homosexual milieu, with its high-strung campery and awareness of social stigma: 'Oh my God, Bruce,' the host asks him, 'why does love so seldom go good for us? We're no worse than other people—no worse and no better ...'

Eventually, Quantock re-encounters the young stranger at another concert and the affair blossoms. It is conducted in secret, in an 'island' of house and relationship, divorced from any wider social stratum. Phillip, the younger man, will not accompany Bruce publicly: 'He implored me not to involve him with my friends, or more precisely my friends of an understood kind. He pictured them in

fact as scornful, rapacious, terrifying; he would instantly find himself one of *them* ...'

'I want to read a novel about queers that treats us as human beings,' muses the character of James Caspar, a novelist who possesses the same first name and initials as Courage. 'I've never understood why murder's considered a proper subject while love between two men isn't ... Hardly any English novelist dares to tackle the subject of physical love; he's too damned scared somebody may catch sight of his balls in the process.'

A Way of Love certainly tackles the subject but its central relationship does not end happily. Phillip meets a man of his own age with whom he has an affair. The end of Bruce and Phillip's relationship is accepted fatalistically by Bruce. Despite Phillip's subsequent attempt to rekindle the romance, it is Bruce who refuses.

The novel ends with a 'generational twist' strangely similar to that recounted in Paul Bowles' earlier short story 'Pages from Cold Point' (1950), where a father–son relationship turns incestuous, or Frank Moorhouse's later novella 'The Ever-Lasting Secret Family' (1980), where homosexual relationships are observed as a continuum in a conservative political context, compromised fathers giving up sons for a similar initiation. In the wake of the breakup of his relationship with Phillip, Quantock is asked by his sister to act as a parent or adviser to her problematic teenage son. Perceiving this as 'something valid because neutral in desire', Quantock accepts the role. Its avowal of neutrality more than hints at its explosive antithesis and forbidden consanguinity.

A Way of Love was reviewed in Landfall in June 1959 by novelist M.K. Joseph, who unjustifiably described it as 'a quietly ruthless exposure of the pretentions of homosexuality, and a sad book despite its appearance of an urbane and sensual exterior'. In 1961 it was banned from shops and libraries on the grounds of indecency and lack of 'redeeming literary merit'.

Courage would publish one more novel before his death in 1963, but since then he has largely remained a forgotten figure in New Zealand literature. New Country: Plays and stories, published by Jeffrey Vaughan's Genre Books, provides a long-overdue re-examination of both the man and his writing, focusing particularly on Courage's homosexuality. The book contains an introduction by Christopher Burke, along with two short plays and five short stories. They are illustrated by a number of Courage's private photographs and related images. The concept, management and project design are credited to historian Chris Brickell.

In contrast to Burke's fascinating biographical examination of Courage in his PhD thesis, 'Speak to me, stranger: Subjectivity, homosexuality, and preliberation narratives in James Courage', his introduction to New Country is more workmanlike. It usefully frames the texts in terms of Courage's sexuality, but it is without the flares of detail that fascinate a non-academic reader. It also begins the book's somewhat tantalising habit of gesturing towards Courage's 14 private diaries, held by the Hocken Collections. Burke refers to these diaries as 'one of the greatest single resources for reconstructing a queer New Zealander's evolving sense of self': a statement that makes a good case for their future publication. This, however, is small solace to the reader of New Country, who is presented with tempting fragments of these diaries, as quotes and artful page-holders in a book otherwise filled with covert identities and masked same-sex desire.

The works gathered in New Country cover the range of Courage's career. Some are published for the first time, others have been previously collected. 'Guest at the Wedding', one of the more accomplished stories in the book, was originally published in Landfall in 1954 and concerns a party of young people holidaying on Stewart Island, which Courage visited in 1935. The narrator falls in with Harry, already engaged to Enid. There are shared confidences and hopes. A moment of nude bathing becomes a Lawrentian wrestle between the narrator and Harry on a beach:

'What on earth did Harry and you think you were? Scrapping on the beach like that? A couple of ancient Greeks?'
'Why ancient Greeks?'
'Well, you know what they were. Hot stuff in the wrong way.'

The story ends bathetically when, after an interval of months, the narrator returns to Invercargill for Harry's wedding to Enid, gets drunk, and at the end of the night manages to blurt, 'Take me with you—I can't live without you—I love you,' before falling into a bed of dahlias, surrounded by laughing wedding guests.

'Scusi', again from *Landfall* in 1954, enters the same world of repressed longing, hanging on the edge of spoken acknowledgement. Francis, a retired naval commander and widower, lives with a young Italian servant in a house on a promenade on the British south coast, 'now what he'd always fancied he'd been at heart, a celibate'. His servant has been a POW of the Germans, cannot cook, and has only a rudimentary knowledge of English. The two men are isolated, locked together by their roles, without real communication. The only moment of physical contact is a sympathetic kiss on a cheek in the wake of Francis' mother's death, followed by his reactive blow against the servant's intimacy. It is a carefully nuanced recounting and a fine story, filled with density and shadows.

New Country usefully reintroduces an unjustly neglected New Zealand writer, and provides significant context for a much overdue reassessment. Courage's stories, at their best, equal the posthumously published short works of E.M. Forster that similarly deal with homosexual desire.

Words and literature can be a means of transmitting a homosexual sensibility in a near-genetic way, coding same-sex desire in the genome of the language. Courage's *A Way of Love* succeeded in this task admirably. It was frank where Sargeson wasn't. It seemed designed to nurture a self-aware and self-generating community. *New Country*, however, is a curious book, its contents completely defined by its ordering subject, and the selections gathered without qualitative measure. Juvenilia and mature works are given the same status. It approaches a clinical symptomology rather than a satisfying compilation. The best short stories of *New Country* seem test-runs for *A Way of Love* and suffer by comparison. Revealingly, 'Scusi' seems to be the book's most admirable text in a literary sense, precisely because the subject of homosexual desire is buried so inextricably deeply in the narrative that the repression itself becomes the shining lure.

Young, Urban, Tragically Hip

by Tim Jones

ShameJoy, by Julie Hill (Giant Sparrow Press, 2014), 130 pp, $24.95

As I write this, my house is surrounded by dinosaurs. It's late afternoon, a time when dinosaurs gather, and I have only to open the front door to hear them chirruping away to one another, or see them gathered, silently, on the wires. From the back porch I can see a bold dinosaur watching me from its vantage point on the topmost branch of the neighbours' tree, a ruff of white feathers bobbing at its neck.

So I'm going to abandon the metaphor I too easily reach for when it comes to new authors and new publishing ventures: that of small, adaptable mammals seeking out and occupying new niches as the industry's dinosaurs blunder above, oblivious. Because the birds, the avian branch of the dinosaurs, are with us still, and what is Giant Sparrow Press, which has published Julie Hill's first collection ShameJoy as its first book, if not a bold new dinosaur on the block, glamorous of plumage and beady of eye?

ShameJoy is something of a swift, feathered beast itself. It alights, pecks, seizes a juicy morsel of story in its beak and flits away. It is curious, agile and omnivorous: it feeds on the decline of Generation X and the rise of the Millennials.

And it is funny, something that New Zealand books rarely aim for and even more rarely achieve. The humour comes from a mixture of verbal wit and absurd situations, as the characters start wars, quest for unusual body modifications, and generally pinball around off one another.

The first story in the book is strategically placed, as it tackles a topic that almost any Kiwi will identify with and also provides a fine introduction to Julie Hill's comedic skills. 'The Pavlova Debacle' tells of a war between Australia and New Zealand that erupts from a much more serious dispute—over the origin of the pavlova. When combative Tauranga-born expat Uncle Jeff takes out a full-page advertisement in *AdelaideNow*, announcing New Zealand's claim to the pavlova in language that no true Australian could take lying down, the result is a trans-Tasman conflict that puts even Anzac Day rugby league tests in the shade.

That's the beginning of the action but not the beginning of the narrative: Hill opens with a scene in which Tony Blair's government, angered by the murder of an envoy Britain has sent to broker peace in the 11-year conflict, decides to have Antipodeans in London rounded up. The year is 2000:

> They found us on the Tube, on our way to our quasi-legal working holiday jobs: back end of donkey in the new Jason Donovan panto,

through a friend of Jason's cousin; fill-in section editor at *The Guardian*; clown doctor, earning hundreds and thousands of the mighty British squid.

Standing silently, balancing against poles, staring at advertising, reading Metros, trying to merge into our environment like lizards. We never spoke because our accents would have given us away.

Absurdism founded on a base of closely observed realism is what makes this story of the differences between Australians and New Zealanders, and their common helplessness in the face of Tony Blair, work so well. But you have to pay attention when reading these stories: the elements of the narrative are all there but not necessarily in linear order. Julie Hall's film and theatre background comes out in the snappy writing and swift changes of viewpoint that help to make the stories in *ShameJoy* memorable.

Another of my favourites is 'Catastrophist of Newtown'. Now, to be fair, I'm predisposed to like it because the city end of Newtown is about 15 minutes' walk from where I live and it's a suburb I pass through quite often. Locational factors aside, however, this is a sprightly and elegant story that takes that stock character of New Zealand realist literature, the man alone (mentally disturbed, isolated, emotionally maladjusted) and makes him and his milieu interesting again through smart writing and clever story construction. Hapless protagonist Con calls an old flame:

'Hi Nancy, this is Conrad Jablonski.'
'Oh my God.'

'How are you?'
'Fine, Con. Why are you calling?'
'I just wondered what you're up to these days.'
'Working at the optoelectronics centre. Like before.'
'What are you working on?'
'It's complicated.'
'Go on, I'm interested.'
'Ridge wave-guides in lithium niobate by differential etching following spatially selective domain inversion.'
'Right. Are you well?'

Because I have read a lot of stories by a lot of authors about these guys (and—confession time—even written one or two), I thought I knew exactly how this one was going to end—and then it didn't. It finished on an unexpected grace-note.

I'm not sure whether it's a criticism of *ShameJoy* to say that most characters fall within a fairly narrow spectrum. They're young, they're urban, they're hip—at times, tragically hip. They're all about that inner-city living, that overseas experience, that metropolitan flair. With the notable exception of poor Con above, few of them could legitimately include either the School of Hard Knocks or the University of Life in their LinkedIn profiles.

Clearly these are characters, and types of characters, that Julie Hill knows, and she writes about them very well. When she strays from them, the characterisation and the humour become less assured: the one character in 'The Pavlova Debacle' whose scenes didn't work well for me was Christopher Morley-Watkins, the negotiator charged by the Tories with ending the trans-Tasman war prior to Tony Blair's intervention. Christopher comes across as a character from Central Casting, a generic weak-chinned Hooray Henry, so his scenes don't have the humour derived from close observation that is so effective in the rest of the story.

The last two stories in the collection, 'Ich Bin Don Juan' and 'The End', showcase *ShameJoy*'s many strengths and occasional weaknesses. 'The End', set in the Ireland of Patrick Kavanagh and James Joyce, is one of the longer stories in the book, and here I found the rapid changes of scene and viewpoint became a little wearying: there are just too many characters and scenes introduced in too close a succession, even though the central throughline remains interesting. (I would be interested to see how well the technique would function in a novel-length work.)

'Ich Bin Don Juan' is again set among expats, this time in Germany, where the young of many lands have flocked together to learn the tongue of Schiller and Goethe. National stereotypes—the arrogantly oblivious Republican, the 'perfectly timed Swiss'—are both reinforced and subverted.

In 'Ich Bin Don Juan', the short scenes play off against a consistent narrative viewpoint, and the whirl of characters ceases before it loses the power to intoxicate. The ending will be familiar to anyone who has shared a short but intense experience—acting in a play, say—with a band of relative strangers:

On the train platform, we all embraced and promised to see each other again. But we knew we never would.

I'd like to see more of Julie Hill's writing—and I hope Giant Sparrow Press brings us more exciting and diverse new fiction. Fly on, freshly fledged friends.

Under the Spell

Kathryn McCully

Grace Joel: An Impressionist Portrait,
by Joel L. Schiff (Otago University Press,
2014), 176 pp, $45

I am a reader, and those of you who are also readers will know that books engage us in an experience over a period of time, the best ones an engrossing conversation or immersive narrative that, like any experience, can transport you from the dull confines of everyday routine to another realm in which we may see the world and our place within it afresh. A good writer establishes a relationship with the reader, and when successful we feel the loss of this relationship upon reaching the final pages. What kind of experience we are about to embark on is often the most intriguing when little is known of the journey ahead. In 1981 mathematician Joel L. Schiff encountered and was struck by an artist's work exhibited at the Auckland City Art Gallery. Enamoured by the artist's 'impressionistic manner', Schiff conducted further research and gathered what little information he had collected in a folder he labelled 'Grace Joel'.

Over the following four decades the folder's contents grew, until in 2010 Schiff decided to discover what he could

about a painter he describes as 'relatively unknown', and provide context to his belief that Joel has not been adequately recognised for her significant contribution to painting in New Zealand.

It is with the intention to put together the pieces of Joel's life to document her rightful place in New Zealand's art history that Schiff takes the reader on a tour of sorts through a collection of material that serves as evidence in a chronological account of Joel's life titled *Grace Joel: An impressionist portrait*. Schiff's interpretive, evidence-based approach is punctuated by his own personal observations, thoughts, and on occasion what he acknowledges as assumptions about Joel's life and work. These latter provide refreshing interludes throughout a book that can be otherwise dense and somewhat unrelenting in its adherence to chronology, which begins with Joel's birth in 1865 to Maurice and Kate Joel, and her early years growing up in Dunedin; and concludes with her death in a London nursing home in 1924. Schiff's comprehensive account of the life of an artist is contextually rich, interpreting and incorporating a broad range of material, including newspapers, diary entries, letters, catalogues, periodicals, photographs and so on related to the time and the communities that may have shaped Joel and her painting practice.

The front cover has attracted a lot of interest as I have carried the book around, and worked in various cafés, libraries and classrooms. I have noted that the female nude still captures viewers' imaginations. The cover painting, titled Nude with Fruit (1920)—Joel's relaxed, reclining, fair-skinned nude with eyes downcast, perhaps surveying the fruit she grasps—seems to welcome the viewer's gaze.

Nudes, according to Schiff, were 'problematic' in the 1920s and 30s, with few exhibited, and many of Joel's deemed risqué, as evidenced by an Otago Daily Times review: 'Some of her works, little seen in her life time and still privately owned, are frankly erotic in their approach.' Schiff supports his assertion that they were contentious by referencing Joel's Reclining Nude, which he writes was also identified by Sandra Chesterman in her 2002 book, FigureWork: The nude and life modelling in New Zealand art, as significant and serving to trace 'the sexual maturity of the nation'. In this painting, a bare-breasted woman floats as if asleep or dreaming in a dark pool surrounded by cherubs, one of whom appears to be captivated by its own reflection in the water. In 1893, during her time at the National Gallery School in Melbourne, Joel became the first woman to be awarded the Ramsay Prize for painting the nude. Apparently the depiction of the nude figure by a woman was considered 'scandalous', provoking 'outraged citizens' to lobby through newspapers to stop life-drawing classes and prevent the exhibition of students' works.

For myself as a graduate of Dunedin's School of Art, and for those of my generation who made the decision to go to art school but found it still difficult to pursue a career in the arts, it is clear that Joel was in a privileged position. While Schiff discusses Joel's family as being of modest means, Grace's father Maurice owned the Red Lion Brewery, and despite having to pursue numerous court cases for defendants' non-payment of ale supplied, the family lived in a stately two-storey home originally built in 1863 for a Polish prince, and were active members of a 'burgeoning mercantile society'. Joel was provided for sufficiently not to have to rely on the sale of her work but was 'free to pursue her artistic endeavours as and where she liked'. Although Joel, according to Schiff, 'neither lived nor travelled as extensively on the continent as her compatriot Frances Hodgkins', she spent and produced work over a summer in Étaples before returning to London in 1901, where it was her 'intention to remain permanently in the artistic profession', with an annual income from her father.

Joel became a working member of the Otago Art Society in 1886, and it is speculated that on her return from studying in Melbourne she may have met and become involved with artist Girolamo Pieri Nerli, who came to Dunedin to assist with the New Zealand and South Seas Exhibition. Joel's contribution to the annual Otago Art Society exhibition in 1890, titled Under the Spell, depicts a young woman resembling Joel posed deep in thought—pondering, Schiff surmises, the future of art and of

Nerli. Nerli, also a working member of the Otago Art Society, established his studio in the Octagon and taught at the Dunedin School of Art, during which time he was undoubtedly an inspiration to students and the wider arts community. One of the 11 paintings Joel contributed to the society's 1896 exhibition is singled out by Schiff as bearing a 'highly suggestive title': *The Dead, Dead Past is Gone; The Present.* Perhaps, the author suggests, it is no coincidence that Joel painted Nerli's portrait and that Nerli left Dunedin 'without fanfare late the same year'.

Schiff's commitment to the research, preservation and interpretation of the life and work of Grace Joel documented in *Grace Joel: An impressionist portrait* will be a lasting legacy to New Zealand art's historical canon. Even though it is apparent there are numerous references and bodies of knowledge associated with Joel, Schiff has drawn together an admirable diversity of resources that, through a collage-like process, evokes an evolving picture of a prolific New Zealand artist deeply engaged in a community of practice from which she drew support, friendship and inspiration. Schiff's 'portrait', as the title suggests, is a study equally imbued with his desire to explore the age and influence of Impressionism. He also draws comparisons between an impressionist approach and his own in the writing of the book, stating: 'Some parts of the image are as sketchy as a Matisse; other parts have more detail, as in a Manet. But there are no regions as

finely painted as a Bouguereau.' And while he is clearly not an art history native, Schiff's passion has resulted in an honest, comprehensive and enlightening account of the career of a neglected artist. It offers the opportunity for any one interested in New Zealand art to become better acquainted with a significant early painter.

Lost in the Hokianga

by Andrew Paul Wood

Taheke: An account of the Hokianga in the life of New Zealand painter Annette Isbey, by Denys Trussell, with photographs by John Miller (Brick Row, 2015), 60 pp, $35

Before reading this book I had only been vaguely aware of Annette Isbey, a shadowy outlying presence not fitting tidily with any particular lineage of New Zealand art and some uncertain memories I had of classical profiles and Byzantine or Gothic countenances glimpsed in some publication or other, a knack for stone-like textures necessitating a Google. For the most part they hold up very well: the stylised and impassive hieratic faces of Quattrocento severity that distantly echo the work of Tony Fomison; the austere formalist landscapes in cool and muted palettes that would be comfortable rubbing shoulders with similar work by Rita Angus or Leo Bensemann. Born in 1927 and with 50 years of exhibitions under her belt she is still painting away in her studio in Auckland's Westmere and good on her.

Denys Trussell is, of course, a well-known rooster of New Zealand letters: poet, biographer, essayist, musician and ecologist. His books on A.R.D. Fairburn and artist Alan Pearson are exceptional pieces of biography as literature, and I am particularly fond of his essay 'Nature and the Pākehā: Finding a way in Oceania', which looks at the melanin-challenged tribe's relationship, its paradoxes and nuances, with this part of the world through art and literature. His literary contributions to the environmental cause are taonga of the global movement.

What one first notices about this book is that it's very short at 60 pages and reads as if Trussell originally intended it as an article for *Art New Zealand*, but then recycled it and padded it out with a lot of intrusive meditations on the landscape, tangents on Māori spirituality, and even entire poems (including one of Trussell's own) with tenuous connections to whatever is being discussed at the time, to the point where, in places, Isbey seems almost incidental. It is, to say the least, indulgent. Some writers can make this sort of psychogeography work—Martin Edmond, W.G. Sebald or Iain Sinclair for example—but here one is left with the feeling that a jolly good no-nonsense editing was called for. Also, for an artist who is not perhaps as well known as she might be, one might expect many more illustrations of her work to be included rather than the three or four that actually are present to tantalise and leave hungry.

Unambiguously the Hokianga, that history-larded estuarine valley, is the biographical subject. In fact I'm not entirely sure why Trussell pegged it to Isbey at all (those curious about the artist's work are directed to Richard Wolfe's essay in *Poetic Vision: The art of Annette Isbey* (Emerson Publishing, 2013) or the 2012 interview in Trussell's documentary film series on New Zealand artists, *Cultural Icons*, produced by the Depot ArtSpace in Devonport). The book opens with Isbey's Depression-era childhood on an undercapitalised dairy farm in the Hokianga at a time when the area was only marginally more accessible than the moon. We lose Isbey for a bit in an exegesis on the significance of the Hokianga as the turangawaewae of Ngāpuhi and as the landing place of Kupe (a slightly jarring experience, as while Isbey obviously has a deep spiritual connection to the area, neither she nor Trussell has any apparent whakapapa to Ngāpuhi to warrant quite such a grand tour without acknowledging the fact or contemplating the complexities of identity). There's a nice bit of poetic landscape porn, an evocative prose sketch of Isbey's farming childhood, and then it's up and off to dally with Isbey's aunt, Gwen Hawthorn, apparently because of her close friendship with Robin Hyde. Then, before we can catch breath and digest this tidbit of information, we are whisked off to Isbey's teenage years and this is how things more or less carry on for the entirety.

There are more vivid sketches, and when Trussell is on point he is a very capable essayist. We learn about (though nowhere near as much as we would like) Isbey's close friendships with local Māori, her mother's ambivalence about her artistic ambitions, and the treatment of her near-fatal peritonitis by the local

doctor at Rawene Hospital, the gifted Scottish surgeon and intellectual George 'Hokianga' Smith. This gives Trussell opportunity to go off on another tangent: the good doctor's eccentricity, his flowing mane (earning him the soubriquet 'Tenei te tangata pohuruhura' from local Māori—the man with the long hair), and steady stream of New Zealand cultural figures he attracted to the area (Olivia Spencer Bower and A.R.D. Fairburn are name-dropped). The significance is not really apparent as Isbey did not interact with these notables and indeed barely with Smith himself. Thence a brief mention of Augustus Earle and Charles Heaphy visiting in the Hokianga in the nineteenth century as a rather long-jump lead-in to artist Eric Lee-Johnson's presence there in 1947–48 (not that Isbey seems to have actually had anything to do with Lee-Johnson, but apparently she had 'contact' with his art—whatever that means exactly). Then fast-forward to the 1970s, long after Isbey had left the area, and the hippie influx, then present day and a brief mention of artist Allen Gale at Waiotemarama and then backtracking to Isbey starting at the district high school at Kaikohe.

It's here at the midpoint of the book (although close to the end of the actual text) that things begin to get meaty again: Isbey remarking at the time, the absurdity of learning French at school when it would make much more sense to be learning Māori, for example. It is here that we learn the significance of the book's title, *Taheke*, in relation to the landscape of the Hokianga and in Isbey's landscapes. As well as being the local marae, citing the old Herbert Williams *Dictionary of the Maori Language* (first published in 1844 and still largely unsurpassed) Trussell informs us:

> Its sharp yet beautiful dissonance spells the living of water. The verb 'taheke' is 'to descend or drop as a liquid'. As an adjective it suggests 'quick' or 'precipitous'. As a noun it is a waterfall.

The magnificent Taheke Waterfall is, of course, a popular Hokianga tourist attraction and features as the subject of a number of paintings by Isbey which Trussell gives a totemic significance. Alas, we do not linger long.

World War II comes and goes in the space of two pages, and in 1946 Annette leaves the Hokianga, marrying in 1952 Eddie Isbey, MP and later under-secretary for Labour for the Kirk government, who didn't mind her being a painter 'as long as she did the house work as well'. There the biographical narrative ends and a short discussion of Isbey's large 2007 triptych of the Taheke falls furnishes a sort of coda.

The discussion is, however, from an art historical perspective, a vacuous muddle of pseudo puffery, namedropping Kandinsky, Mondrian, Cézanne, Colin McCahon, Wittgenstein, Taoism and tikanga in a very generalised way that actually does little to illuminate what is at the heart of Isbey's vision—the irreducible essence of form in the landscape. At only one point do we get a

sense of what Isbey actually thinks about art, in relation to some notes she made on a Francisco Zurbarán (1598–1664) painting, *Still Life with Lemons, Oranges and a Rose* (though failing to furnish the painting's date, 1633) at the De Young Museum in San Francisco (presumably on loan from its home in the Norton Collection in Pasadena). The uncanny stillness, inertness, austerity and solidity of forms in the Spanish baroque artist's work seem to have affected her, but even then all we are presented with are some notes copied from the museum catalogue. It is strange that in all the talk of 'presentness' in the art, in the flurry of philosophers no one thought to mention Heidegger, who might actually have been relevant.

Ultimately we are left with what looks like a potentially interesting book on the Hokianga that should have been much longer, into which a short biographical essay on a minor senior New Zealand artist has been shoehorned (or vice versa) as a kind of stalking horse, largely to the detriment of both. Trussell's enthusiasms run riot, and indeed run over Isbey's tenuous presence in the text, which seems to exist only to push the narrative along by virtue of her having lived somewhere or vaguely known someone. The few pages expended on Isbey's artistic interpretation of the Hokianga—which the title would suggest is the raison d'être for this publication—are far too general and superficial to provide any significant understanding. The index barely seems justified. It's a wafer-thin after-dinner mint of a book that doesn't seem to know what or where it's going; either not concentrated or not expansive enough— just somewhere frustratingly in between. That said, it still manages to suggest the dense poetic and historical texture of the place and of Isbey's roots there.

WAITAKERE CONTEMPORARY GALLERY

JAMES COUSINS:
RESTLESS IDIOM

29 November 2015 – 21 February 2016
Opening Saturday 28 November, 4pm

teuru.org.nz

LOPDELL   **Waitakere Ranges Local Board**

future Landfall editor swots up

UNITY BOOKS

VUP 2015

The lives of Joan Riviere and Hermann
Henselmann form an incomplete history of
Europe's 20th century in these two novellas.

fiction, August, p/b $30

A hilarious and troubling satire on the
making and manipulation of literary fame,
by the author of the acclaimed novel *Gifted*.

fiction, October, p/b $30

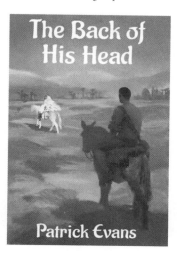

Ocean and Stone is elemental Dinah
Hawken, at once meditative and resolute.

poetry, September, p/b $35

This is Bill Manhire as backyard inventor,
devising stories in which the fabulous and
the everyday collide.

fiction, November, h/b $40.

vup.victoria.ac.nz

EMILY KARAKA, Settlement

At Old Government House in Auckland on the 12th February 2010 Emily Karaka was the first iwi representative invited to sign the Manawhenua O Tamaki Makaurau and Crown Framework Agreement under which hapu and iwi would negotiate settlements of their historic treaty grievances against the Crown. Two years later at the Auckland War Memorial Museum the Manawhenua O Tamaki Makaurau Collective Deed of Settlement and Post Settlement Governance Proposal was signed by Emily Karaka and representatives of ten hapu and iwi and the Minister of Treaty Negotiations, on behalf of the Crown.

The Tamaki Collective Deed, which sits alongside hapu and iwi specific settlements, includes the transfer of ownership of 14 maunga (mountains), 3 permanent motu (island areas including the tihi - summit of Rangitoto), ownership of specific motu and Right of First Refusal over all surplus Crown owned land and certain Crown Entity owned land within Tamaki Makaurau for 172 years.

On the eve of Ngai Tai ki Tamaki's settlement, Emily Karaka's exhibition Settlement explores the Crown's settlement process, old land claims and Turton Deeds transactions that alienated lands and islands from the Tribes of Tamaki. As a descendant of Kiwi Tamaki (who resided on many of the volcanic cones in Tamaki) and a descendant of the Ngai Tai Rangatira Nuku (who participated in land sales deeds and signed Te Tiriti O Waitangi at Karaka Bay in Auckland in 1840), the artist confirms: Ka Mau Mahara – we will remember.

orexart WWW.OREXART.CO.NZ   rex@orexart.co.nz

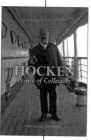

CONTRIBUTORS

Airini Beautrais lives in Whanganui. Her most recent book of poetry is *Dear Neil Roberts* (VUP, 2014).

Andrew M. Bell writes poetry, short fiction, plays, screenplays and non-fiction. His work has been published and broadcast in Aotearoa New Zealand, Australia, England, Israel and the USA.

Philip Braithwaite won the New Zealand Young Playwrights' Award in 2000, the BBC World Service/British Council International Radio Playwriting Award in 2001, and the Adam NZ Play Award for his play *The Mercy Clause* in 2013. In 2013–14 he was the William Evans Playwriting Fellow at the University of Otago.

Liz Breslin lives and writes in Hawea Flat, near Wanaka. Her poems have been published in *Landfall*, *Takahē*, the *Otago Daily Times* and *Bravado*. She was second runner-up in the 2014 NZ National Poetry Slam. Her website is www.lizbreslin.com

Kay McKenzie Cooke is a Dunedin writer. Her third poetry collection, *Born to a Red-Headed Woman*, was published by Otago University Press in May 2014.

Brett Cross lives on the edge of the Hauraki plains in the Waikato, where he manages the two small presses Titus Books and Atuanui Press.

William Dart is a composer, broadcaster, writer and critic. Formerly a senior lecturer in the music department at the University of Waikato, he reviews music for the *New Zealand Herald* and is editor of *Art New Zealand*.

John Dennison was born in Sydney in 1978, and grew up in Tawa. He now lives with his family in Wellington, where he is a university chaplain. His first collection of poems, *Otherwise*, was published by AUP and Carcanet in 2015. He is also the author of *Seamus Heaney and the Adequacy of Poetry* (Oxford, 2015).

Kieran Doody is a poet born and raised in Christchurch. He currently resides in Porirua.

Lynley Edmeades is a PhD candidate at the University of Otago, looking at poetry as a sonic art. Her poems and reviews have been published in New Zealand and abroad, and her first collection of poetry will be published by Otago University Press in January 2016.

Murray Edmond was formerly associate professor in drama at the University of Auckland. A poet, and the editor of online journal of poetics *Ka Mate Ka Ora*, his most recent collection of poems is *Shaggy Magpie Songs* (AUP, 2015). He has worked has an actor, writer and director for numerous theatre companies, including Mercury Theatre and Town and Country Players.

Riemke Ensing lives in Howick, Auckland, and is the author of 12 collections of poetry, most recently *O Lucky Man: Poems for the Charles Brasch Centennial*, (Otakou Press, University of Otago, 2009). Canterbury University composer Alex van den Broek is presently working on a chamber ensemble setting for her volume *Storm Warning: After McCahon*. Early in 2015 she held a writer's residency at the Caselberg Trust house in Broad Bay, Dunedin.

Nod Ghosh graduated from the Hagley Writers' Institute in Christchurch. His short stories or poems have appeared in *Takahē*, *Penduline*, Christchurch *Press*, *The Gay UK*, and *Flash Frontier*.

Rogelio Guedea, born in Mexico in 1974, is the author of more than forty books, including collections of poems, essays and stories. He also writes crime fiction. A columnist for several Mexican newspapers, he is currently the coordinator of the Spanish programme at the University of Otago.

Bernadette Hall's tenth collection of poetry, *Life & Customs*, was published by VUP in 2013. Recently she has been a guest performer at Dunedin and Christchurch book festivals and in Golden Bay, Nelson and Lyttelton.

Michael Harlow's books of poetry include *Giotto's Elephant*, *Cassandra's Daughter*, and *The Tram Conductor's Blue Cap* (AUP, 2009), shortlisted for the NZ Post

Book Awards in 2010. He lives and works as a writer, editor and Jungian therapist in Alexandra. He has been awarded the Peter and Dianne Beatson Fellowship for 2016.

Jeffrey Harris is a self-taught artist who grew up on a farm on Banks Peninsula. He has worked with Colin McCahon, Ralph Hotere and Tony Fomison. He lives in Dunedin.

David Herkt is an Auckland writer and reviewer. He has edited a number of New Zealand gay publications including *express* and *JACK*, and has written extensively on homosexual issues. He is a multi-award-winning television director and researcher.

Roger Hickin lives in Lyttelton and is a visual artist, poet, translator, book designer and publisher at Cold Hub Press. He translated into English Rogelio Guedea's poetry collection, *Si No Te Hubieras Ido / If Only You Hadn't Gone* (Cold Hub Press, 2014).

Jeffrey Paparoa Holman is a Christchurch poet, historian, memoirist and reviewer. His books include *Best of Both Worlds: The story of Elsdon Best and Tutakangahau* (Penguin, 2010) and *Shaken Down 6.3* (Canterbury University Press, 2012).

Derek Jones is currently working on 'The Great New Zealand Novella', the second installment of his *Anonymous Author*

series. He lives at Waiwera, north of Auckland.

Tim Jones is a fiction writer, poet and anthologist. He was co-editor of *Voyagers: Science fiction poetry from New Zealand* (2009) with Mark Pirie, and his books include the poetry collection *Men Briefly Explained* (Interactive Publications, 2011) and most recently the novella *Landfall* (Paper Road Press, 2015)

Emily Karaka was born in Auckland in 1952 where she continues to live and work. She belongs to the Tāmaki Makaurau hapū (sub-tribe) of Ngāi Tai. Karaka has exhibited regularly since 1980 and cites artists Colin McCahon, Philip Clairmont, Allen Maddox, Ralph Hotere and Tony Fomison among her mentors.

Erik Kennedy's poems have appeared in *Catalyst* and *Sport* in New Zealand, and in various publications in the US and UK. He is poetry editor for *Queen Mob's Teahouse* and is on the board of *Takahē*. Originally from New Jersey, he now lives in Christchurch.

Fiona Kidman has written novels, short stories, memoirs and poetry. Her latest novel is *The Infinite Air*. She has won several awards over a long writing life. Her home is in Wellington.

Leonard Lambert's latest collection is *Remnants* (Steele Roberts, 2013). His *Selected Poems* is about to be published. He lives in Napier with fellow poet Jan FitzGerald.

Therese Lloyd is a Wellington poet and writer. Her first full-length book of poetry, *Other Animals*, was published by VUP in 2013. Formerly the administrator at the Adam Art Gallery, she is currently pursuing a PhD in creative writing at Victoria University of Wellington.

Olivia Macassey's writing has appeared in a number of New Zealand journals. She is the author of two books of poetry, *Love in the Age of Mechanical Reproduction* (2005) and *The Burnt Hotel*. She lives in Whangarei.

Philip Madill is a Dunedin-based artist who recently completed his Master of Fine Arts with Distinction at the Dunedin School of Art.

Ria Masae is a student at Manukau Institute of Technology, studying for a Bachelor of Creative Writing degree. She was a finalist in the 2014 Going West Festival Poetry Slam, and the 2015 Auckland Writers' Festival Poetry Idol.

Kathryn McCully is programme manager in visual arts, film and animation at the Southern Institute of Technology, Invercargill. Previously, she was manager/curator at Ashburton Public Art Gallery.

Carolyn McCurdie is a Dunedin writer of poetry and fiction. Her first collection of poems, *Bones in the Octagon*, was published in April 2015 by Mākaro Press as one of their Hoopla 2015 series.

Andy McKenzie lives in Christchurch. His writing has been published in *JAAM*, *Takahē* and *Landfall*.

Cilla McQueen was the New Zealand Poet Laureate 2009–11, and her most recent collection of poems is *Edwin's Egg and Other Poetic Novellas* (Otago University Press, 2014). She lives in Bluff.

Courtney Sina Meredith was the Bleibtreu Berlin Writer-in-Residence in 2011. Her play *Rushing Dolls* was selected for Silo Theatre's Working Titles programme in 2015. At present she is working on *Tail of the Taniwha*, a book of short stories, with support from Creative New Zealand, and she has a writing residency at the Sylt Foundation (Germany) in 2016.

Hannah Mettner is a Gisborne writer who lives and works in Wellington. She has had work published in *Sport*, *Hue & Cry*, *Turbine*, *JAAM*, and *Cordite*. She is one of the editors of the new poetry journal *Sweet Mammalian*.

Alice Miller lives and works in Vienna. She held the Grimshaw Sargeson Fellowship in 2014, and her first collection of poems, *The Limits*, was published by both Auckland University Press and Shearsman that year.

Paul Moon is a professor of history at the faculty of Māori development Te Ara Poutama at Auckland University of Technology, where he has taught since

1993. His specialist areas of research include the Treaty of Waitangi and the early period of Crown rule in New Zealand. He has written several books on aspects of New Zealand, including *Encounters: The Creation of New Zealand*, published by Penguin Books in 2013.

Tony O'Brien is an Auckland poet. He lectures in the faculty of medical and health science at the University of Auckland.

Peter Olds lives in Dunedin. His many collections of poetry include *You Fit the Description: The selected poems of Peter Olds*, published by Cold Hub Press in 2014.

Nicole Page-Smith is a regular contributor to the Harris Smith Art Museum Blog: harrissmithart.blogspot. com/2015/08/what-british-recommended.html

Jenny Powell is a Dunedin writer who has published six individual and two collaborative collections of poems. Her most recent collection is *Trouble*, published by Cold Hub Press in 2014.

Joanna Preston is a Tasmanaut poet and freelance creative writing tutor living in semi-rural Canterbury with a flock of chooks and an overgrown garden. She is the current poetry editor of *Takahē* magazine.

Nicholas Reid is an Auckland historian, critic and poet. His poetry collection *The*

Little Enemy was published by Steele Roberts in 2011. His second collection is currently with the publishers.

Alan Roddick was first published in *Landfall* in 1956. Recent work by him has appeared in *Tintean* and *Eureka Street* (Melbourne), and *The Scottish Review of Books*. He lives in Dunedin.

Jack Ross's latest book, *A Clearer View of the Hinterland: Poems and sequences 1981–2014*, appeared in 2014 from HeadworX. He teaches at Massey University, edits *Poetry NZ* and blogs at *The Imaginary Museum*: http://mairangibay.blogspot.com/

Martin Rumsby is a writer, independent film-maker and film historian who lives in South Auckland.

Emma Shi was the winner of the 2013 National Schools Poetry Award and is currently studying at Victoria University of Wellington.

Peter Simpson is an Auckland-based writer and critic. He is currently editing a two-volume selection of Charles Brasch's journals 1946–73 for Otago University Press.

Tracey Slaughter's novella *The Longest Drink in Town* was published in 2015 by Pania Press. Her short story 'Scenes of a Long-Term Nature' won the 2014 Bridport Award, and her next collection of short fiction *Deleted Scenes for Lovers* will be published in 2016 by Victoria University Press. She teaches at the University of the Waikato.

Robert Sullivan's books include the long-poem *Star Waka* (Auckland University Press), and the New Zealand Post Children's Book of the Year, *Weaving Earth and Sky*, illustrated by Gavin Bishop. With Reina Whaitiri, in 2014 he edited the first comprehensive anthology of Māori poetry in English, *Puna Wai Korero* (AUP). He is head of Manukau Institute of Technology's creative writing school.

Mere Taito is a Rotuman Islander from Fiji, living in Hamilton. She moved to New Zealand in 2007 and works as an instructional designer at the Waikato Institute of Technology. She writes when time is kind.

Louise Wallace's essay in this issue was written while she held the Robert Burns Fellowship, 2015. Grateful acknowledgement is due to the University of Otago for this support, and thanks also to friends Chris Tse and Lynley Edmeades for feedback on earlier versions.

Yiyan Wang migrated to New Zealand in 2012, and she currently lives and works in Wellington.

Andrew Paul Wood is a Christchurch-based art historian, writer and critic who contributes to a wide variety of publications.

CONTRIBUTIONS

Landfall publishes poems, stories, excerpts from works of fiction and non-fiction in progress, reviews, articles on the arts, and portfolios by artists. Written submissions must be typed, with an accurate word count on the last page. Email to landfall@otago.ac.nz with 'Landfall submission' in the subject line, or post to the address below.

Visit our website www.otago.ac.nz/press/landfall/index.html for further information.

SUBSCRIPTIONS

Landfall is published in May and November. The subscription rates for 2016 (two issues) are: New Zealand $50 (including GST); Australia $A52; rest of the world $US53. Sustaining subscriptions help to support New Zealand's longest running journal of arts and letters, and the writers and artists it showcases. These are in two categories: Friend: between $NZ75 and $NZ125 per year. Patron: $NZ250 and above.

Send subscriptions to Otago University Press, PO Box 56, Dunedin, New Zealand. For enquiries, email landfall@otago.ac.nz or call 64 3 479 8807.

Print ISBN: 978-1-877578-91-5
ePDF ISBN: 978-1-927322-52-9
ISSN 00–23–7930

Copyright © Otago University Press 2015

Published by Otago University Press, Level 1, 398 Cumberland Street, Dunedin, New Zealand.

Typeset by Otago University Press. Printed in New Zealand by Printlink Ltd.

Philip Madill, *Embodied Agents*, 2013, 76 x 56 cm. Graphite on paper.